Neil Young and his use of Native American imagery in the sixties

Stephen M. Catchpole

ISBN:8799579995
ISBN-13:9788799579990

DEDICATION

The Long and Winding Road beckons us all.
This book is dedicated to the ones who took that road.

CONTENTS

ACKNOWLEDGMENTS

The contents of this book are completely unauthorized. The assumptions and conclusions that have been made and drawn by me are the result of analysis from films, books, magazines and records that are in the public domain.

There is no connection between the historian Stephen M. Catchpole and any of the people or companies mentioned in this book. The Hippie Trilogy of which this book is number two was compiled from four years of research made for the history dissertation in 2009, 'Neil Young and his use of Native American imagery during the 1960's.

All authors and works have been cited where appropriate.
My thanx to the Rusties and other people who contributed to the research.

NEIL YOUNG.

The image that Neil Young projected in the sixties through his work and music was enhanced by his dress code and the outlook he expressed onstage and in interviews. On the released CD of one of his live shows from 1968 "Showboat,"[1] one can hear during the banter with the audience how he creates this intimacy, he talks about incidents in his life that the audience can relate to. He expresses a feeling that was universal for young people at that time and very reflective of the 1960's. It gives an atmosphere of; no-one could really see where life was heading but they believed it was heading to a better place and they were enjoying the ride. A large proportion of people who were young back then will tell you there was no better place to be than sitting in the intimacy of a performance by an acoustic artist. We should also remember that artists like Neil Young, Bob Dylan, and Leonard Cohen were showmen and entertainers as well as musicians and social critics. They and others left an undeletable mark on the second half of the twentieth century. The songs and music made by these troubadours has had a profound effect on many people's lives. It brought pleasure back then and is now associated with memories of youth. Today these songs are tucked away in the recesses of the mind and bought out in moments of reflection. Besides helping people to cope with certain periods in their lives, artists like Neil Young have in many cases been an influence in helping them to make life changing decisions. In this context his music really becomes a part of their personal 'soundtrack' that accompanies them down life's highway. I was 'on the road' in Europe when Neil Young's 'Harvest' came out and whenever I hear a track from that LP, I am transported to the side of some hot and dusty road in Italy. Many people have these musical moments, as Pete Townshend once commented: *"you should remember the first time you heard the opening bars to 'Jumping Jack Flash' and cherish those moments for the rest of your life."*

The association between Neil Young and Native American imagery in his work has always been there. It is intriguing that one still associates him with traditional Native American imagery from the Old West despite the fact that he stopped dressing up as an 'Indian' in 1968. This is partly due to promoters still connecting him with the Old West on his tour posters and record covers. Feathers, spears and broken arrows in fact any Native American theme seems to have a natural affiliation with the name Neil Young. This is also partly to do with him being Canadian coming from a place where First Nation people live. Graham Nash uses the image of a tepee for the cover of his collection box set, here I think it would be more appropriate to have images like the ones in the opening titles of 'When the Boat Comes in' or something more Mancunian. However it could also be Mr. Nash now feels more spiritually connected to the Old West. When examining the connections and interactions from that time to try and appreciate the effect they might have had on the way we live today we really have to consider the sixties and the music made back then as 'real history'. In that period Neil Young was a key player and a critical member of the team. He was in the forefront of what was going on personally and artistically. He can be associated to some of the most seminal events connected to popular music and culture during those exhilarating times. He was without a doubt right in the eye of the storm that was shaking the music world. Here are some examples of how important the band he formed with Stephen Stills in 1966 called The Buffalo Springfield were. Directly after they formed they toured with the Byrds. They opened for the Rolling Stones at the Hollywood Bowl in July 1966 (albeit without Neil Young at the event). Neil Young appeared with Buffalo Springfield in the program and posters for the Monterey Pop festival but again he was associated with the event but not actually there in person. However he did make it to Woodstock the event that has become the high water mark and reference point for the whole 60's generation and became their symbol of hopes and dreams for a new world. The slogan of "Three days of Love and peace" promoted popular rock music and the hippy ideal to the mainstream. Young people from the counter culture showed that it was possible for "half a million young people living together side by side and just grooving". Today the whole concept might be regarded as a utopia but it did happen, half a million people put theory into practice. Woodstock the movie gave millions of people outside the US (myself included) the possibility to share the experience. In the UK that meant you got the atmosphere of an American music festival first hand in a very social environment. Smoking in cinemas was still allowed at that time and many people passed 'cigarettes' around as they dug the music. I can still remember the buzz I got from seeing the film at Leicester Square. For me 'The Who's' performance struck a personal chord as I had gone through my teenage years listening to them on the radio and together with the Kinks they are representative of a distinctly English dimension in the rock music of that period. The opening sequence with The Who where you see Roger Daltrey gastrulating amid an eruption of tassels from his jacket is a good example of how a long tasselled jacket can really enhance a live performance. They give the effect of power in the physical movement, the flurry and raging fury. Sly and the family Stone gave an amazing performance at Woodstock clad in very flashy tassels. It is easy to see how a tasselled war shirt would enhance a Cheyenne warrior in battle. It would give the arms a silhouette of wings when they are outstretched in an attacking charge. At Woodstock Neil Young wore a frilled white shirt. His appearance in the film is not very noticeable because he refused to be filmed onstage because it distracted him from his music but at least he was there this time! It is important to remember that a decade is not necessarily only defined by actual dates. The vibe or build up to when people adopt the trends can start before the actual number 1960 appears on the calendar and there were still prominent remnants of major aspects of what the sixties represented after

2

the decade officially ended. Musically and culturally with films like 'Woodstock' (and political events like Vietnam which ended first in 1975). When Woodstock was released in 1970 things were still very vibrant concerning music generally and with Neil Young's particularly as he released some of his most memorable music during that period. Another film with a mega rock soundtrack was 'Easy rider' released in 1969 here the motorcycle replaces the horse in a modern Western where the outlaws sold drugs instead of robbing banks. The film was a road trip showing an alternative lifestyle that transported the American dimension of the sixties round the globe. As actor director Denis Hopper[2] said "We'd gone through the whole 60's and nobody had made a film about anybody smoking grass without going out and killing a bunch of nurses. I wanted 'Easy Rider' to be a time capsule for people about that period." A forerunner to this film and another Hopper, Fonda collaboration called "The Trip" the film plot is a simulation of the main character played by Fonda taking his first LSD trip. The films soundtrack by Electric Flag is a good example of psychedelic music from the period. Despite being a commercial flop at the time it does show some of the values people had. When CSN&Y were asked by Peter Fonda to contribute to the soundtrack they heard it and replied "what for? It's perfect". Like Altamont, Easy Rider ended tragically. If Woodstock in August 1969 was the high point of the sixties Love and Music era, then the Rolling Stones free festival four months later at Altamont in December of 1969 was the abyss where everything started to go into a downward spiral. At Altamont a member of the audience moving towards the stage with a drawn gun was stabbed to death by Hells Angels. Crosby Stills Nash & Young were also on the bill and one of the members of the Jefferson Airplane was knocked out by a Hells Angel. The film today generates a dark and satanic feeling. You can clearly see many people appear to be suffering the effects of heavy drugs, alcohol and bad acid. David Crosby recalled "we just went in and played and got out, the atmosphere was extremely heavy". With the benefit of hindsight it is easy to see using Hells Angels for policing an event where there is liberal use of drugs and alcohol was probably not the wisest of decisions. Although it had worked for the Stones previously at their free Hyde Park concert. Altamont went desperately wrong showing the pitfalls of creating an alternative security. Most people today would probably opt for the legitimate law enforcement agency as opposed to an alternative one made up of an outlaw motor cycle gang. However one must remember that the American police during this period used extreme violence at the slightest opportunity against the counter culture and demonstrators singling out especially young long haired people and African Americans. This was regardless of how peaceful the demonstrations were. As a consequence of their behaviour the Police became affectionately referred to as PIGS in the USA. Another aspect we can see

3

with hindsight is that aside from groups like the Weathermen and Black Panthers most young people in general did not want the downfall of Western society. They wanted more personal freedom to determine how they should lead their lives. They wanted freedom from the confinements of a generally militaristic attitude to upbringing that was being forced on them with preconceived gender roles. In the UK for example during the sixties all people of lower social status were addressed by their surnames. It was like being in the bloody army.

Before 'Monterey Pop' the only acceptable music festivals had been Classical Music, Jazz and to some extent traditional folk music. The concept of a 'Pop Music' festival had never been tried before. So it could have easily turned out to be 'Monterey Flop' and pop music festivals would have ended there, but because of its success the British followed by organizing the first Isle of Wight Festival, (1968) booking top acts like Hendrix, Dylan and the Who. This would happen repeatedly during the sixties, the status quo in the entertainment industry could not predict the trends in films and music. The market demands dictated the direction and film directors and musicians in the entertainment business supplied the demand. Low budget films like "Easy Rider" and Spaghetti Westerns achieved success compatible with the big budget movies made in Hollywood. Musical artists took more control over the production of their work. The roles were in many cases reversed instead of producers directing musical bands and orchestras as they had done in the past. Rock artists and other performers dictated to producers the sound they wanted to create. Ever since the early days of Rock bands like the Beatles, Stones and The Jimi Hendrix Experience gave their sound priority over their dress style and fashion image. This became even more evident as the bands became more and more involved with the mixing and producing of their own records. Neil Young and Stephen Stills were not satisfied with the production of their first Buffalo Springfield album and decided they had to learn more about the technical production process of recording. Neil Young had a recording studio built into the cellar of his house in 1968. Private recording studios became the norm among the rock elite. Traditional recording studios and methods of production appeared confining and in some cases technically inadequate. Hendrix designed his state of the art recording studio 'Electric Ladyland' in New York to accommodate his recording ambitions. This enterprise nearly broke him financially and because of this he was forced to continue a gruelling schedule of live dates. The Beatles stopped touring at the time of Sergeant Peppers to totally dedicate themselves to creating music in the studios. For their creative endeavours they had unlimited access to EMI's recording studio. Bob Dylan booked a studio in Nashville for a 14 day block to record his masterpiece 'Blonde on Blonde'. This had never been done before and the slightly amazed session musicians sat around playing cards and smoking cigarettes while Bob finished off writing songs. They grabbed what sleep they could in between takes. This autonomy spread into other areas of the entertainment industry when actors like Jack Nicholson and Clint Eastwood achieved prominence, they stared producing and directing their own films. Up until that time plastics and synthetics were all the rage and dominated fashion and design in mainstream culture. Now something started happening in the entertainment industry where people were no longer willing to be puppets or marionettes, artificial elements in the construction of their work. They wanted to take charge of their own destiny even at the expense of losing popularity as was the case with the Monkees whose record sales plummet when they started to insist on playing their own instruments. After they turned down 'Sugar Sugar' it was recorded by the Archies a totally synthetic animated cartoon band. After that the Monkees lost their position as one of the top bands in the US. The counter culture started to associate more and more with natural products and authenticity. Many young people started to prefer clothes made from natural materials tie dyed by hand. The Beatles sanded down their Epiphone guitars to give a natural wood finish on the Revolver album. The British invasion was a major factor to changing the format from solo artists to groups in the States. Giving the opportunity for musicians like Neil Young and Stephen Still's to form a band and 'get on the bandwagon.'

To do this research I created what I call a "Neil Young History Tree".

At the base of the tree would be what was happening in Canada and in the world when he was born. What were the things that influenced him (and others during that time?)

In the roots would be what was happening when his parents and grandparents were born. These events would be within living memory of the people around him as he is growing up. How deep do the roots of the tree go? Particularly concerning the history of the Native Americans and how their way of life had been portrayed at that time.

The branches on the tree, the closer you get to the trunk the more connected things are to events happening in his life. This includes of what was around him while he was growing up and any big events or changes in the society. Other events that had a big influence at the time move farther from the stem as time and their relevance passes. But they are all there growing in the tree. Some branches close by others far away but all connected and feeding from mother earth through the roots and breathing through the leaves.

What were on the branches around him when he formed a band with Stephen Stills in L.A.? Counter Culture? Beatles? Civil Rights Movement? Hippies?

The main focus is on his work in that period particularly with Buffalo Springfield and on Native Americans.

How Native Americans had been portrayed in films up to that time and how they were represented in Western Culture.

Finally, I firmly believe that if we are to get an understanding of the sixties, it is the duty of teachers and amateur family historians, school classes and others to document that period in history while the people who lived through those times are still with us. That is what brings history alive, being able to relate to it.

If you want to write about a band from back then try and find someone in your family who saw them and interview them. Write it down for prosperity, tell your grandchildren about it, put it online.

If you are serious about doing something like this either as a classroom assignment or as an independent research project it is important to start with one piece of hard evidence for example a family photograph from the period or a primary source like an album cover.

I have tried to focus my research on specific areas and one of the main ones is the visual record of Neil's use of Native American imagery on album covers, photographs, films, tour posters (from that period and contemporary ones.)

For the written works about Neil Young I have looked at;
Biographies, sleeve notes, magazine articles and internet web sites like "Thrasher", "Rust List" and CSN&Y "Lee Shore", these are internet discussion groups and websites where fans of Neil Young and CSN&Y exchange information and stay connected.

BUFFALO SPRINGFIELD TAKES OFF!

The Buffalo Springfield were very much a product of their times. To understand them it is necessary to understand how they came about and what their situation was. Practically all five members had a track record going back to adolescence notably Neil Young playing in High schools bands like 'The Squires' then the folk circuit in Toronto along with the likes of Joni Mitchell and Buffy saint Marie and finally together with bassist Bruce Palmer in the Mynah Birds. Stephen Stills sang harmonies in different groups along with Ritchie Furay and played the folk circuit in New York. He first met Young in 'Blind River' while doing a minor tour of small clubs in Canada in 1962. The drummer Dewy Martin was the only one with any significant experience playing with bands that had any commercial recognition as he had played with the Dillard's and Eddie Cochrane. Each of them had some musical experience, they knew how to play and sing. But they had no preparation as a band for what was to come. Much has been attributed to the internal conflicts within the band as the reason for the final brake up after two short years. The limited experience they had as a band playing together before they became known would also have been a relevant factor. They had only practiced for one week before their first engagement, which was as support band touring with "The Byrds " who at that time were one of America's top acts. Compare their beginning to The Beatles who had 10,000 hours of live performance under their belts before they even began recording.[3] When the Buffalo Springfield formed, Rock and Roll was a very established and sought after commodity. Despite not having the long apprenticeship of other bands from the very start Neil Young, Stephen Stills, Ritchie Furay, Dewey Martin and Bruce Palmer had hit the ground running, writing their own music and creating their own stage image of the 'Old West'.

Despite not achieving the desired chart success during the period of 1966 – 1968 Buffalo Springfield gave Neil Young his first exposure to a wider audience through records, radio and TV. This period established the beginning of his fan base, which would increase in numbers and follow him throughout his career. During his period in The Buffalo Springfield Neil Young continued to develop his highly individual guitar style and voice. His voice and guitar solos from the Buffalo Springfield first album are distinguishable as the roots of his later style. After hearing Bob Dylan's unmusical voice Neil Young was inspired to sing his own compositions. Richie Furay sang lead vocals on Neil Young's first composition 'Nowadays Clancy can't even sing' that was released as a single by The Buffalo Springfield. After that Neil always sang his own material. During this period with the Buffalo Springfield Neil Young's music and persona received their first substantial commercial exposure. His image was projected through concerts, television and fan magazines and his very special idiosyncratic sound a high pitched voice accompanied by a rough distorted electric lead guitar started to reach a wider audience.

The group was formed by Americans Stephen Stills and Ritchie Furay who met Canadians Neil Young and Bruce Palmer in LA in 1966. They needed a drummer and enlisted another Canadian, Dewey Martin. The story goes that Neil Young was in LA looking for Stephen Stills as his career at that time seemed to be going nowhere. According to Neil Young they were too young to handle the fame and pressure of constant media attention that Buffalo Springfield soon attracted. This and conflicting egos contributed to the bands demise after two years and three commendable although not commercially strong selling albums.

During their first tour with The Byrds Stephen Stills was introduced to David Crosby one of the Byrds founding members. Buffalo Springfield went from strength to strength appearing on television getting coverage in teenage magazines and supporting the Rolling Stones at the Hollywood Bowl. They played a sixth month residency at the infamous "Whiskey a Go Go" in LA that was considered by many of the band members as their musical high point. The albums and recordings of TV shows from that period are evidence that The Buffalo Springfield were extremely good. The performances show that they played country rock and 'shook the cage' like lots of other rock bands were doing at that time. The TV shows also expose the popular Cowboy Western Clothing this reinforces the evidence that the Buffalo Springfield were the originators of the Country Rock dress fashion and brought a purely American image of cultural heritage to pop music. Unfortunately they did not achieve the full commercial success they deserved. Had they got that recognition the band might have taken a different course? Ahmed Ertegün had constantly supported their aspirations and like Epstein with the Beatles he believed in them. He believed in their potential to be a big success and was supportive to CSN signing them to Atlantic and he was the one who suggested bringing in Neil Young as lead guitarist. Time is sometimes on the side of the artist and the recognition CSN&Y later received outshone anything Stills and Young had previously achieved. The Buffalo Springfield was posthumously recognized for the group's contribution to music in establishing the Country Rock sound when they were inaugurated into the Rock and Roll Hall of Fame. Old publicity shots of the Springfield portray Neil Young and the others in Union Calvary uniforms or cowboy clothes. On stage and on album covers Neil is wearing Native American clothes from that period in American History. Neil Young always championed the rebels and the outsiders and for a period after Ritchie Furay´s wedding, he wore a Confederate Calvary uniform.[4] As Mark Volman states "No one was going around in Comanche war jackets and Indian beads or Confederate uniforms until the Springfield"[5] These clothes were much more authentic looking than the exaggerated stage outfits traditionally used by Country and Western bands. The year 1967 was the Summer of Love and the music industry throughout the Western world was soaring to unprecedented popular and commercial heights. Music and especially rock music was an integral element of the counter culture. Airplay and the accessibility of transistor radios made a vibrant atmosphere everywhere people congregated. This was the music of youth and it crossed cultural and social boundaries. There was an enormous following that was not only limited to the counter culture. Young draftees took it to Vietnam and it became the soundtrack of the decade. In war zones and at space launches Rock was the background music signifying how far people had progressed or digressed. Rock became the soundtrack to the visual image of daily life in the sixties. The Buffalo Springfield's first breakthrough single "For What it's Worth" was protest song about what they saw was going down in society. The Beatles were five years older than Stills and Young when Revolver came out one can clearly see they were paving the way determining the way music was going. The Buffalo Springfield acknowledges their debit to them on their second album naming Ringo as an inspiration. The Beatles single 'Hey Jude' clocking in at over seven minutes long broke the mode of the 2½ minute single. Songs became more extended and longer. Buffalo Springfield's tracks are noticeably longer on the second album some were musical collages like Neil Young's 'Brocken Arrow'. It is possible the Buffalo Springfield could have challenged the Beatles if they had stayed together. They were an outstanding live Rock and Roll band, who according to Stills: "blew the Rolling Stones away when they played support band to them at the Hollywood Bowl".[6] At the Hollywood Bowl in front of 19,000 screaming Stones fans Neil Young was in his fringed Buckskin Jacket while Bruce Palmer wore his Indian motif in beaded moccasins and fringed chaps. The others wore neatly-trimmed suits.[7] This was the image of the Buffalo Springfield that the fans knew and loved. It is easy to say in retrospect how things might have been but the reality was that the second album which is now considered a minor masterpiece only reached number 44 in the US charts and failed to make an impact anywhere else. The posthumously released, best of album 'Retrospective' went platinum and proves without a doubt the potential was there but the recognition came too late. Within a year of Buffalo Springfield breaking up Stills formed Crosby Stills and Nash which achieved the chart success that Buffalo Springfield were denied after Young joined them making CSN&Y they evolved into what was termed "Super group". Young and Stills, who were the creative axis of the Buffalo Springfield along with contributions by Ritchie Furay, continued to be the creative mainstay of CSN&Y. One obviously cannot ignore the presence of David Crosby and Graham Nash, these two veterans of chart topping bands: The Byrds and The Hollies made a considerable contribution to the quartet.

Not least in their songs and amazing harmonies that are one of the hallmarks of CSN&Y's sound. Their songs have become classics and they achieved considerable recognition with their solo albums. But Stills and Young were the outstanding creative elements. They never co-wrote songs but neither did Lennon and McCartney they each wrote them individually and then registered them as dual efforts because as Paul McCartney states in the 1987 TV documentary by Tom Sheppard: "that's the way we had always done it."[8] To illustrate the longevity of Buffalo Springfield's legacy their second single "For what it's worth" made the charts and became one of the most recognizable anthems of the sixties. Their first album that was hastily reissued with the single on it had a very unique fresh sound where one can clearly detect the beginnings of Country Rock and hear Stephen Stills and Neil Young's strengths as composers and singers. Unfortunately the mixing of the record left a lot to be desired. The second album was pure Country Rock that clearly showed the potential of the band: "Bluebird" captures Stephen Still's music style and "Mr. Soul" captures Neil Young's hard rocking drive. This album was released one year before the Byrds "Sweetheart of the Rodeo" which is considered a seminal Country Rock album. Buffalo Springfield's third album 'Last Time Around' is not considered by Neil Young to be a group effort as the group had effectively split up by the time it was released. It is a collection of songs by the individual members. Neil Young used some of these songs on his solo tours at that time and renditions of it can be heard on the CD of the 1968 concert 'Sugar Mountain-Live At Canterbury House' that was released in 2008 For this reason Neil Young did not include the 'Last time Around ' album on his Archives box set covering the period.[9] The Sugar Mountain CD clearly shows Neil Young was capable of holding an audience enthralled. Without any backing band and performing an acoustic set. When the Buffalo Springfield finally split up Ritchie Furay formed Poco with Jim Messina who had replaced bassist Bruce Palmer on various occasions and produced the final Buffalo Springfield album. Steven Stills formed CSN with David Crosby formally of the Byrds who stood in for Neil young at the Monterey festival and Graham Nash from the UK band The Hollies. Neil Young was already honing his skills as a solo artist during the making of Buffalo Springfield's second album with producer Jack Nietzsche who produced "Expecting to fly" and 'Brocken Arrow'. He released a solo album with orchestral accompaniment on most of the tracks. This first solo debut is not typically Neil Young his idiosyncratic sound which has now become his trademark first appeared with his second album "Everybody knows this is nowhere" which he made together with Crazy Horse. Despite the fact it did not receive good reviews in Rolling Stone magazine at the time, where it was unfavorably compared to his first album. Time has proved it to be a masterpiece.

BANDS AND NAMES.

It is fascinating when you see that many of the American Rock Bands in the sixties and seventies adopted names that could have easily been taken from Native American Warrior Societies. These include The Buffalo Springfield, The Byrd's, The Eagles and Rodger McGuinn's Thunderbird.

In the UK one might consider the Animals or the Beatles as names associated with nature. The name for the band 'Beatles' came to John Lennon in a dream with instructions to spell it with an 'ea' and not a double e.

The origins of Buffalo Springfield are not so romantic although it could be said that the name appeared as a blurred vision to the band as they were coming home one night.
The story goes that in 1966 the band saw the name of a construction company 'Buffalo Springfield' on the side of a steam roller in LA.

The Buffalo is one of the mightiest animals in the Native American culture and is known as the Thunder Beast.

Of all these names the Eagle is the most powerful and in the 19th century Eagle feathers were very valuable to Native Americans.
A full series of 12 feathers could be traded for a pony and only warriors who had experienced battle were allowed to wear them.
The record "The Eagles Greatest Hits" became the biggest selling record of all time. The name of the band is usually a very personal statement, sometimes using the member's names or something that has special relevance to the group. US bands could draw on cultural images like Buffalos and Thunderbirds that were indigenous to America.

The English did not really have any equivalent to this in their recent history. We could not go round dressed as Desert Rats and Paratroopers using the names of famous regiments for our bands! The closest they got to that in the UK was the fashion craze of wearing military uniforms, the jackets in particular. This popular trend of wearing dress uniforms originated in the 'Kinky Clothes' shop in the Portobello Road in 1967.[10]

THE NATIVE AMERICAN ASPECT OF BUFFALO SPRINGFIELD.

Neil Young's representation of the Native American aspect of Buffalo Springfield is reinforced by fellow Canadian Bruce Palmer. As a Canadian the artist Neil Young used Native American imagery in his work most notably in his formative years as an artist in Buffalo Springfield. It was during these first 5 years of his career that his personal use of Native American imagery is most prominent. It appears later on album covers but he does not wear it again onstage after Buffalo Springfield.

What images does the name 'Buffalo Springfield' conjure up in the minds of those not initiated into the world of construction and hard hat terminology? The group liked the sound of it and adopted the name for their band. The Buffalo had an immense status and role in the identity and mythology of the Plains Indian. They are associated with Buffalo hunts and Medicine men who wore Buffalo horns as a head dress. For the white settlers it was a fixture on the plains that was initially used to feed railway workers and later had to be eliminated to make room for domestic cattle that would become America's staple diet.

The secondary effect of wiping out the Buffalo was to subdue the Native American population who were literally dependent on them for survival. The success of this annihilation of the herds is evident by the surrender of Crazy Horse in 1887 after the battle of the Little Big Horn. Most of his followers were literally starving after searching the plains for months in vain for food.

Neil Young raises a herd of Buffalo on his ranch that he rents out to films like 'Dances with Wolves'. The image of the Buffalo was used again in 1972 when Stills and Young formed the "Stills, Young Band" on the cover of the LP "Long May You Run" there is a pair of Buffalo from an old drawing. The cover itself is made to appear like a framed picture from the previous century. On the back of the cover is a drawing of a piece of string to hang it up on.

In 1980 Neil Young worked on the soundtrack of a film called: "Where the Buffalo Roam" based on Dr. Hunter S. Thompson's book 'Fear and Loathing in Las Vegas'. This book is a 1960's classic that was first serialized in Rolling Stone with illustrations by Ralph Steadman. This book epitomized the drug culture from that period and showed the literary attributes of 'Gonzo Journalism'. Neil Young did the orchestral arrangements for the film and wrote three of the songs "Buffalo Stomp", "Ode to Wild Bill" and "Home, Home on the Range" based on a the traditional song that was once considered for the American national anthem. The song opens with the merry lines: "Oh give me a home where the Buffalo roam, where the deer and the antelope play. Where seldom is heard a discouraging word and the skies are not cloudy all day". A fitting eulogy to the Old West, images of bygone days when animals moved freely across the plains.

The Buffalo remains a majestic beast no matter where you see it. Even roaming through the long grass of Northern Germany [11] as the sun sets the European Buffalo evokes an image of the Old West.

Neil Young and his production team have cultivated this image to such an extent that it is automatically recognized and accepted by his fans today. A tour poster illustrated with a War Bonnet or any kind of Native American motive seems in perfect harmony with the artists name. The other half of the name 'Springfield' evokes an image of something growing and blooming. Spring is the time of year when things spring up out of the ground and grow as nature comes into bloom. The resin rises in trees. Spring is a popular time for people to fall in love. Animals shed their winter coats and start to mate, nature takes its course. A field has many functions and symbolic meanings. It can be where you plant things or hold a battle. A field of vision or experience marks people's boundaries. It has spiritual meaning as in 'The Soldier' by Rupert Brooke "The corner of some foreign field" and biblical "He layeth me down in green pastures". To take time out and lay down in a field on a sunny day or a field covered in snow and gaze up at the sky can give you a special feeling as you watch the world go by. In American culture settlers had to clear fields to plant crops it was a prerequisite for survival that goes right back to the early puritan settlements.

The Buffalo Springfield was the originators of "Country Rock" not only the music genre but the image as well. They were dressing up in regalia from the old west before any other bands. They utilized props and clothing from the old west on their record covers and Neil Young incorporated Native American themes in his songs. It is my contention that this reemergence of images of the Old West in the film and music industry contributed to the cause of the Native American civil rights movement. The increased exposure came from the counter culture using Native American dress and the films released during that period along with the Country Rock bands performing live on TV and on the covers of teen magazines. This bought Native American aspects of visual images and language into popular usage: band names like "The Buffalo Springfield" and "Crazy Horse" conjure up images of the Old West. Song titles like "Broken Arrow" and "Cowgirl in the Sand" takes the general public's collective imagination back to the period in history known as the 'Wild West'.

So did Neil Young's use of Native American clothes on stage help to bring the Native American theme into the public eye and thereby help to 'demystify' their culture? Even if there is no hard evidence of Neil Young taking any concrete action. The reproductions and Native American regalia he wore was historically accurate enough to have some effect on the viewer consciously or subconsciously he would associate seeing these clothes with the Old West of 1890. This was the period when the armed struggle against the Native Americans was coming to an end and a major historical event the closing of the frontier was taking place. This was the end of the colonization process and the end of the Native American way of life. From then on basically except for some isolated events during WW1 and WW2 the situation in America for the Native Americans and the African Americans (over whose emancipation the Civil War was fought over in 1865) had laid dormant until the sixties when the Black civil rights groups started to organize and fight for their rights en masse under the leadership of Martin Luther King. These developments inspired Native Americans to organize themselves and some of the young Native Americans saw the militant actions of the Black Panther movement as necessary at that time to achieve their rights. They organized the group AIM and pledged to lay down their lives if necessary in the fight for Native American civil rights and land rights. I combine these two groups in American society because injustice has no colour. Injustice against any group of people in any society is an injustice to all mankind and should not be accepted or tolerated. You cannot approve of one group against injustice and let another group go on suffering unrecognized. Concessions have to be made and in the sixties these causes became interrelated. Here Neil explains how he adopted the stage image. At the time it appears to have been purely the showman's view of "that looks cool." There was apparently no ulterior motive.

"There I was making 120 bucks a week at the Whiskey as a musician," explains Neil on how his identity unconsciously developed. "I´ve always liked fringed jackets. I went out and bought one right away with some pants and a turtle neck shirt. Oh yeah, I thought I was heavy. I wore them on some TV shows and whenever we worked. Then I went to this place on Santa Monica Boulevard near La Cienega. I saw this great Comanche war shirt, the best jacket I've ever seen. I had two more made. The group was Western, the name Buffalo Springfield came off a tractor, so it all fit. I was the Indian. That´s when it was cool to be an Indian"[12]

This is evidence of Neil Young's interest in Native American clothing as he describes the jacket as the "best jacket I've ever seen" and the fact he orders two more means he already plans to use them extensively. He wore them on "TV shows and whenever we worked" This was his image and he was the originator. He was ¨The Indian in the group¨ before the term existed. He returns to the subject two years later in an interview with Rolling Stone journalist Elliot Blinder. Here Neil Young is describing the pressures of working with Crazy Horse and CSN&Y simultaneously, the journalist asks: " Is that a reflection of what was in "Broken Arrow," of being a rock and roll star?

To which Neil replies; "Yeah, that was when I was living in Hollywood, though, that's a whole other number I was into then. I was a Hollywood Indian" to which the journalist replies somewhat taken aback "You were?"

and Neil replies, "I guess so, everybody thought I was an Indian. That was when it was cool to be an Indian. I was wearin` fringe jackets and everything. I really loved these fringe jackets I used to have with the Springfield. I dug wearing them." "What happened then" the journalist asks to which he replies: "They died with the Springfield. A lot of changes went down in everybody's heads when the group broke up".[13]

Statements made in magazine interviews usually reflect what the artist was concerned about at the time the interview was taking place, as opposed to a memoir where they will look back and reflect. In this interview, Neil is obviously very tired from touring with Crazy Horse in between commitments with CSN&Y as he talks about maybe doing something else as he is 24 years old at that point and says: "I'm getting tired of this too. Really it's groovy but I don't know how much longer I can do it." To make my point; Neil Young has continued for another four decades right up to the present day and is still headlining festivals and concerts. Both these statements from Neil Young, one from 1970, the other from The Story of Buffalo Springfield published in 1997 help support one of the main points in my thesis, namely that he cultivated the Indian image to such an extent in the beginning of his career that he was referred to as "Neil the Indian"[14] in fan magazines. Neil says in the interview with Elliot Blinder "Everybody thought I was an Indian". Suggesting it must have been a common occurrence in interviews and presentations. This must mean that the branding and cultivation of that image was so extensive at that time: visually, in his stage clothes as an artist and the images used on the record covers and promotion photographs. Orally: In the name of his band Buffalo Springfield and later when he continues his association with Native Americans by calling his band Crazy Horse and his recording studio and Ranch, Broken Arrow. This firmly cements his connection to the Old West and Native American culture.

It is my contention that the consequence of this association orally and the visually resulted in a natural affiliation between Neil Young's and any 'Western Theme'. A perfect example of this is the concert poster for Neil Young in Firenze from 2006 (see photo supplement) where there is a sketching of a War Bonnet on a brown background with his name underneath. This is despite the fact that Neil Young has not worn Native American clothes since the early seventies, except for the occasional cowboy hat. Magazines do occasionally depict him wearing these clothes in old photographs.[15]

The Buffalo Springfield formed in 1966 which makes them the forerunner of the Country Rock image style as Barry Friedman explains:

"In a time of Nehru suits and British velvet-collared jackets, the Springfield bought an American image to pop music, their very name conjuring up echoes of the Old West, wide open skies, wagon trains, cowboys and Indians. Stephen and Neil deliberately cultivated this look, Stephen appearing in smartly tailored suits and a cowboy hat; Neil appearing at times as a self-styled Hollywood Indian, wearing buckskin jacket with fringes, at other times as a Confederate soldier dressed in uniform".

Later he continues; "I had seen what the Byrd's were doing with their characterizations and their modeling of individual looks and costumes, Each one with his own trademark: David with his capes and McGuinn with his glasses. That's what we wanted to carry through with the Springfield, individual identities". [16]

Neil Young's explanation on how this image came about is more coincidental. He obviously liked the image and it was a time when the counter culture was starting to use Native American symbols. Hence Neil's comment "that's when it was cool to be an Indian" The explanation Neil Young gives illustrates that he appreciated that he appeared "heavy" dressed in these jackets and that's the image he wanted to project to the audience during that period of creativity in his career. It was solidly in tune with the times and what was going on around him but at the same time because other bands were not doing it, he still was able to stand out as something special. Later in the early 1970's it became more standard as bands like New Riders of the Purple Sage, Gary Puckett and the Union Gap and Don Nix came along in historical military uniforms from the American Civil War.

NEIL YOUNG'S USE OF NATIVE AMERICAN IMAGERY.

There were two aspects to the use of Imagery concerning the Wild West period in American History used by Buffalo Springfield in the mid and late sixties. One was the European dimension that covered the American Military, Union and Confederate and civilian Scouts and Cowboys.

The other was the Native Americans in the form of the Plains Indians' mainly from the Cheyenne and the Comanche tribes. Neil Young used all the European costumes: Union soldier, Confederate Calvary, Scout, Cowboy and the Cheyenne regalia in the form of war jackets, moccasins and replica ornaments for example Bear Claws necklaces. There are two main elements in the culture of the Native American plains Indians up to the late 19th century the spiritual in the form of rituals and ceremonies and the Warrior Societies that focused on war and warfare. The two were intertwined and interdependent. The Plains Indians were not farmers they had no 'Harvest' festivals. They were nomadic tribes that survived by hunting Buffalo and other game. Animals had immense significance to the Native American spiritually in that they believe they descended from them and physically in that they were dependent on them for survival and respected their strength, skill and courage. The plains Indians Warrior Societies looked to the animals for spiritual and physical protection. They did this spiritually by using animal names for their societies like Kit Foxes, Mad Dogs, Doves, Bulls and One Horn. The physical aspect was emphasized by using the image on their shields clothes and weapons along with other images of spiritual mythical animals like Thunderbirds. They were physically protected by using hides for their shields and war jackets that were made of animal hide that were adorned with celestial signs. The shields were normally worn on the back and identified their owners by their unique motifs that were often received through visions and dreams.

Like the ancient Greeks and Romans dreams and visions had an enormous influence, many warrior societies would only go on the warpath if there was good omens. A good example of this is Sitting Bulls vision before the battle of the Little Big Horn. Hearing that the fields would be colored blue from the dead bodies of the soldiers the warriors raced into battle some of them half-dressed believing that it was their destiny to win. However they ignored the warning given in the vision not to loot and defile the bodies as was tradition. This would lead to their detriment as the horses and clothing of the 7th Calvary would be easily recognized later and sometimes the perpetrators' were punished. There was the general feeling among Indians that the Wounded Knee massacre and the subsequent murders of Sitting Bull and Crazy Horse were acts of vengeance perpetrated on the Indians that were responsible for killing Custer.

Crazy Horse is celebrated today in an unfinished statue close to Mount Rushmore.

Some warrior societies kept sacred bundles made up of animal parts of entire skins, feathers, hooves and claws. These were considered so powerful that they were hung outside the teepee and only certain members were allowed to handle them like keepers or protectors they had a priestly status. The sacred bundles were taken into battle and on raids by the society who believed the medicine from them would make them invisible or give them acute sight. A good illustration of this is the scene in Little Big man where the ageing blind chief Old Lodge Skins played by the real Chief Dan George walks through the battle down the hill to the river without being harmed.

To us this is unbelievable but such an incident would not be considered as incredible by Warrior Society members, it would be interpreted as big medicine. The Warrior Society had a strict hierarchy concerning rites of passage. Like the youths in ancient Greece they were groomed for warfare and one of the few places to gain honor and prestige was on the battlefield, scars and bullet wounds were highly valued and scalping and counting coup gave status in the tribe to young males.

These warrior societies were militant by nature but they were marked with a strong sense of spirituality and tradition. The rich ceremonial life revolved around dances and rituals, including drumming, singing and prayers to the natural and spiritual worlds.

In Native American history warfare did not start and end with battle but extended into the social life. Warriors purified themselves before and after fighting. There was much dancing and drumming involved in the ceremonies. The women made warriors ornaments and ceremonial garments. After battle they would decorate the scalps and perform scalp dances dressed in ceremonial costumes in honor of their husband's brave deeds. These deeds would be recounted many times at later ceremonies.

The massacre at Wounded Knee in 1879 ended the armed conflict between the US military and the Plains Indians and with the surrender of Geronimo in 7 years later in 1886 the frontier was finally closed. The frontier had always been a symbol of rich possibilities to Europeans and it forms a vital part of the American character. The unconquered Indian Territory presented a challenge for them in their process of conquering the whole American continent through a process of colonization. They not only took from the Native Americans they also took Louisiana from the French and Texas from the Spanish.

As the Twentieth century dawned the US government had created reservations designed partly to let Native Americans live together as a people on their own land and partly to enforce American culture on the Plains Indians through building towns and schools for a traditionally nomadic people. It is at this point that the Warrior Society dances and ceremonies across the whole plains region becomes a way to maintain continuity with the past. Another aspect was since the tribes were now forbidden to go to war with each other they held collective Pow Wows with former enemies here they could recount battles and brave deeds and in some cases hear the fate of abandoned wounded or raiding parties that had never returned. These gatherings became a way to maintain and ensure continuity with the past lifestyles and preserve community identity. This paints a rosy picture but in many cases the situation was not so idealistic. Many tribes had their identity eroded as they were forced to settle on reservations with other tribes that they were not indigenous with. Other tribes did not have the resources or motivation to maintain their culture but fortunately in some cases anthropologists had recorded some of their dances and rituals and they were able to reclaim them in the 20th century.

With the event of the two world wars and the Native American involvement in them many of the ceremonies like welcoming home the veterans and celebrating their participation in battle were reintroduced. Veterans were always honored in Native American society regardless of the political implications and opinion in the American mainstream. WW1, WW2, Korea and Vietnam were all wars that Native Americans served in and when they returned they were all equally honored and held in esteem for taking part in battle and fighting for the mother country. Regardless of the politics when America was threatened or at war the Native Americans were willing to go to her defense. The early settlers suppressed Native American culture and imposed European culture and ideals on America during the colonizing process. In the early sixties when the counter culture was searching for alternative religions mainly from Asia, Gary Snyder tried to show people that Americans already had an alternative religion that was ethnic in the form of the Native American beliefs. Some of the rituals like the drumming and loud poetry reading were adopted by Snyder and Ginsberg at the Pow Wows held in San Francisco. Many hippies did visit Indian reservations trying to find out more about the Native American lifestyle. These rituals helped create a sense of community and traces of them can be seen at Monterey and Woodstock music festivals.

NATIVE AMERICAN THEMES IN NEIL YOUNG'S LYRICS.

All three of Neil Young's contributions to Buffalo Springfield's second album 'Buffalo Springfield Again':

'Mr Soul', 'Expecting to Fly' and 'Broken Arrow', contain thought provoking poetry that conjure up weird mental images that were typical of the times.

For example compare the Beatles lyrics from 'Strawberry Fields':

"Living is easy with eyes closed, misunderstanding all you see".

To Neil Young's lines:

'There you stood on the edge of your feather, expecting to fly.
While I laughed I wondered whether I should wave goodbye."

The songs 'Expecting to Fly' and 'Broken Arrow' are beautiful examples of orchestrated musical collages.

Young's songs are fully representative of the times and stand out on the album where many of the songs have a distinct country rock sound.

On this album Young´s songs lean towards what is happening at the time with Sgt Pepper and Psychedelic Rock.

Neil Young quoted a verse in Broken Arrow as being among the best lyrics he had wrote:

"He saw that his brother had sworn on the wall, / he hung up his eyelids and ran down the hall, / his mother had told him the trip was a fall, / and don't mention babies at all".

Many people including a critic in the New York Times "didn`t understand the message". Neil´s reply to this was; "It´s just an image of being very scared and mixed up" he goes on "the broken arrow is the Indian sign of peace, usually after losing a war. A broken arrow usually means that somebody has lost a lot"[17]

In the chorus of this song there is one of the few examples where Neil Young actually mentions a Native American:

"Did you see them, did you see them? / Did you see them in the river? / They were there to wave to you. / Could you that the empty quivered, / brown skinned Indian, on the banks that were crowded and narrow, / held a broken arrow ?"

Broken Arrow the Native American term for peace appears to have some relevance to Neil Young as he named the ranch where he lives, "Broken Arrow" and also gave the name to his recording studio.

In 1976 the artist James Mazzeo [18] created a large wooden structure of a broken arrow that hung over the entrance to Neil Young's ranch.

In 1996 Neil Young and Crazy Horse released the album "Broken Arrow" the cover is illustrated with Tepees and other Native American images.

Through this repetitive use of the term it is evident that it is special to him. At the time of the recording the American Armed forces in Vietnam used the term 'Broken Arrow' as an emergency signal that meant a unit was in serious trouble and in danger of being overrun and wiped out.

The original track took him about 100 hours to record. The collage of sounds creates thought provoking images, it starts with a wild version of Mr. Soul sung by Dewey Martin to the background of Beatle fans screaming at a Candlestick Park concert this was added later to make it sound live.[19]

The song ends with the sound of a heartbeat fading.

It was released in the UK [20] on the sampler album 'Age of Atlantic'. For many people in Britain myself included this was the first encounter with the band Buffalo Springfield.

LAST TRIP TO TULSA.

As previously, mentioned Neil Young mentions the Native American in his lyrics in the song "Broken Arrow" written while in Buffalo Springfield. The Lyrics on his first solo album are written in the same period. All of the songs on his first solo album are arranged by Jack Nitszche and have orchestral accompaniment except one "Last trip to Tulsa" this is Neil Young the folksinger alone with his Western Guitar. A hard raunchy unpolished sound accompanying dreamlike lyrics leaves this listener wondering if 'Last Trip to Tulsa' is meant to be interpreted as a psychedelic trip. The song is nine minutes long and has six verses of twelve lines. The last four lines at the end of verse three contain these words: "Well I woke up in the morning, / with an arrow through my nose, / There was an Indian in the corner, trying' on my clothes." In these lines the image is of the frontier settlers being raided. In these situations Indians would dress up in the clothes of the victims of battles and raids. It was common practice to wear the clothes like jackets, trousers and hats of killed enemies as trophies of war to show that one had killed an enemy. This practice was also evident in WW1 when troops returned from trench raids wearing enemy helmets. In the case of Hendrix wearing military 'Hussar' jackets he said on the Dick Cavert show that it was not an act of rebellion but an act of continuality, by wearing the jacket he was paying homage to the warrior that had previously worn it. The lyrics to 'Last trip to Tulsa' are very emotional and powerful. Throughout the song the words conjure up Ralph Steadman or Dali like images. 'The servicemen were yellow. And the gasoline was green. Although I knew I couldn't I thought that I was gonna scream.' Or the Daliesque: 'There were two men eating pennies. And three young girls who cried. The West coast is falling; I see rocks in the sky.' The last four lines of verse five show Neil Young's ability to bringing the nature and seasons into the song accompanied by hospitality: "That was on my last trip to Tulsa, Just before the snow. If you ever need a ride there, be sure to let me know." This is reminiscent of Dylan's 'Ballad of Frankie Lee and Judas Priest' also released in 1968,[21] and the content of both albums reflect the sign of the times. Help each other along the way if you can. "So when you see your neighbor carrying' something', / help him with his load, / and don't go mistaking Paradise, / for that home across the road." These examples are the only time in the sixties that Neil Young mentions Native Americans in his work. In that period the association was mainly visual in his dress as can be seen on photographs. The next time he mentions Native Americans in a song is in 1979 with the album "Rust Never Sleeps" here the whole song "Pocahontas" has a Native American title and theme. As every verse has relevance, If you are interested in this theme you should read the inspirational essay 'A College Essay by Kyle Bichan'. [22] Kyle Bichan's main theme is Cortez the Killer but she also covers many of the points I have mentioned in Pocahontas.

POCAHONTAS.

"Aurora borealis, the icy sky at night, Paddles cut the water, in a long and hurried flight, from the white man to the fields of green, and the homeland we've never seen."

Here is a beautiful image of the nature. Gliding over the water at night with the Northern Lights overhead. The Indians are fleeing from the white man being pushed further and further from their homelands that some of the generations have never seen.

"They killed us in our tepee, And they cut our women down, They might have left some babies, Cryin' on the ground, But the firesticks and the wagons come, And the night falls on the setting sun."

This verse describes a massacre like Sand Creek or Wounded Knee. Associations can be made with the scene in the film Little Big Man where babies are "Cryin on the ground".

"They massacred the buffalo, Kitty corner from the bank, The taxis run across my feet, And my eyes have turned to blank, In my little box at the top of the stairs, With my Indian rug and a pipe to share."

Here Neil is referring to the slaughter of the Buffalo Herds that took place to prevent the Indians from living their free nomadic life on the plains. When the Buffalo were gone their source of food had disappeared and they had to resort to living on the reservation getting food from the white man. The other lines refer to their life in the among the whites: banks and Taxis, metaphors for technological lifestyle and progress, but it only runs over their feet. All they have left from their culture is a few artifacts from their ancestors in a box. The Indian rug to keep the physical body warm and a pipe to share for spiritual contentment.

"I wish a was a trapper, I would give thousand pelts, To sleep with Pocahontas, And find out how she felt, In the mornin' on the fields of green, In the homeland we've never seen."

He uses a metaphor of sleeping with Pocahontas for being in that period in history as a trapper on the frontier. His currency is fur pelts as opposed to the "Bank" mentioned in the previous verse. To sleep with Pocahontas is to experience the Native American life and find out how it felt to live at that time. To wake up in the morning in the homeland they have never seen, again a reference to be driven from their homelands and being born on reservations.

"And maybe Marlon Brando, Will be there by the fire, We'll sit and talk of Hollywood And the good things there for hire, And the Astrodome and the first tepee, Marlon Brando, Pocahontas and me, Marlon Brando, Pocahontas and me, Pocahontas."

Here he is sitting round the fire with Marlon Brando who won an Oscar for his role as the "Godfather" in 1972. He caused a lot of media coverage for the Native American cause at that time by sending a Native American Sacheen Littlefeather,[23] to accept it and make a speech to draw attention to AIMs occupation of Wounded Knee at that time and injustices done to Native Americans in the past and their portrayal in Hollywood films. Hence the line "talk of Hollywood". The reference to the first tepee where a family lives and the Astrodome that holds thousands of people.[24]

This illustrates how far engineering and modern technology has advanced in America since the Europeans have come. In the end there is Marlon Brando, Pocahontas and Neil Young sitting around the fire reflecting. Brando is an American icon ever since his early role in 'The Wild One' in 1953 where he played a young motorcycle gang leader he has represented the rebel a man unto himself that is so important to the American outlook. Because it was so controversial the Wild One was banned in the UK for 14 years.[25]

Through her marriage to John Smith Pocahontas represents a unity between the old world and the new. Marlon Brando's protest action at the Oscars really encouraged and lifted the spirits of the Native American defenders at Wounded Knee. Surrounded by the FBI and American military, two FBI agents and two Native Americans had already died in the incident.

Although the Oscar protest was criticized at the time, it drew much needed media attention to the plight of the Native Americans and was an enormous morale booster for the Native American protesters holed up in the government building at the Pine Ridge reservation offices of Wounded Knee.

ENVIRONMENTAL THEMES IN NEIL YOUNG'S LYRICS.

As Neil Young shows in the lyrics of one of the songs on his first album, "Here we are in the Years" saving the environment as a major element in his work. This track was critical of the urbanization of the countryside and city dwellers relationship to the nature, as can be seen in verses two, three and five:

"Go to the country take the dog, Look at the sky without the smog.

See the world laugh at the farmers feeding hogs, Eat hot dogs.

What a pity that the people from the city, can't relate to the slower things that the country brings.

While people planning trips to stars, allow another boulevard to claim, a quiet country lane, it's insane."

I use these examples of Neil Young's 'eco concern' with environmental issues that he voiced in 1968 to show how far ahead of the curve he and the hippies who were advocating preserving the planet really were.

These themes became more prominent during the twentieth century as people and governments came to realize the consequences of treating the planet like you had another one to replace it.

Neil Young has always advocated conservation of the nature and has been a staunch supporter of small farms in the form of a string of "Farm Aid" concerts, pointing out that American farmers did not get all the subsidies that their EU counterparts got and pointing out that a way of life which is an intricate part of the American identity namely working the land, was fast disappearing in the United States.

With his concern for the environment and love of cars Neil Young wanted to make an eco-friendly car that could drive 100mpg and in 2008 Neil Young together with Jonathan Goodwin (of H-Line conversions) converted a 1959 Lincoln Continental into an electric hybrid called the Linc-Volt that outperformed many of the conventional hybrids. [26]

THE FINAL CONCERT & NATIVE AMERICAN BENEFIT.

Country Joe and the fish were one of the biggest psychedelic rock bands in the sixties and early seventies. They played a style of music that became known as acid rock. The style of the lead guitarist Barry Melton has a lot in common with Neil Young's (without the rough edge). Many of the bands at that time played at the same festivals and wrote protest songs like "For what it's Worth." Country Joe and the Fish released "I Feel I'm Fixin to Die Rag" this kind of music became more mainstream as the protest movement and anti-war movement spread throughout the world so did this form of protest music. Country Joe McDonald really utilized the acoustic guitar both in his solo work and his work with the Fish. Country Joe was a Navy veteran and worked intensively with Vietnam veterans during that period as the lead guitarist of the Fish Barry Melton states:

"Sure we continued to play benefits of all kinds. Success never diminished our opposition to the Vietnam War and our support for progressive causes. In some sense the success of Country Joe and the Fish, and that of our musical contemporaries, directly reflected the success of the antiwar movement. As opposition to the war in Vietnam became the cultural mainstream, so did our music."[27]

The contemporaries Barry Melton refers to are bands like Buffalo Springfield and the other bands that took part in the benefit concert at the Blue Law Club. The Buffalo Springfield's final concert was set for May 5th 1968 at Long Beach Sports Arena in LA. It was announced in the media they would play at a benefit for the American Indian held at the Blue Law Club in Torrance LA in the afternoon before going on to Long Beach but they cancelled.[28] This was the only evidence I could find of direct interaction with the Native American cause by the Buffalo Springfield. The bands playing at the benefit were The Jefferson Airplane, Big brother and Holding Company, Pacific Gas and Electric, Buffy St. Marie and several of the Monkees. The situation appears coincidental, but here you have a gathering of some of the best bands around at that time. Many of them connected directly to Stills and Young; Buffy St. Marie knew Neil Young from Canada. The relationships between these musical master craftsmen lasted and they recruited each other for different projects when possible. For example some of Jefferson Airplane along with Jerry Garcia played on David Crosby's memorable "If Only I Could Remember My Name". Steve Stills and Peter Tork had played in the same coffee shops during their musical apprenticeships and were friends. The Monkees might have been a synthetic band but as one of the biggest groups in the US they commanded respect and had influence. They misguidedly recruited Jimi Hendrix as a support act on one of their tours because they sincerely liked his music. Obviously this must have blown a lot of teenybopper minds in an audience who were not really ready for the Jimi Hendrix experience. The Jefferson Airplane and Big Brother had played at

Monterey together with the Buffalo Springfield. All the bands at that time seemed to coordinate and play the same venues and concerts to appease their fans and endeavor to support the various elements of the society that they thought were worthwhile causes. People and especially artists seemed to have a very clearly defined sense of direction in those days. Not just in songs and music but by participating in demonstrations and benefit concerts. Benefit concerts had media coverage that followed sent out a message to the public about the bands political standpoint and many of the fans adopted these values. The more grassroots activities bands participated in the more connect they were to their fans. People back then were really looking for authenticity in the bands they followed. They wanted them to care about the things that affected them and they wanted them to be genuine. Ironically the Monkees demise was due to the fact that they started insisting on playing their own instruments and writing their own material. They wanted to redeem themselves as musicians in tune with the times where people were putting more and more emphasis on authenticity. They could have carried on being the synthetic Beatles but they wanted to be real! This is an integral part of Neil Young's success as an artist. The fact is that many of his fans and followers appreciate him as being sincere and true to himself in the same way people appreciated Jimmie Rodgers and Hank Williams. On a good night when Neil sits up there on stage all alone with his guitar, he can hold the audience enthralled like a true virtuoso of his craft. David Crosby put his finger right on it when he said "Neil Young is a force of nature it is like having the wind in your band." Neil Young is renowned for going his own way and doing what he wants. He refused to just go on repeating the winning formula of his hit album 'Harvest.' In doing so he gained a position among the Rock elite and had the respect of his peers.

During that period in the USA bands would meet socially, the parties at David Crosby's house in LA were immensely popular because of the girls and good quality of the illicit substances.[29] In this way they kept each other informed about what was going on. In the same way artists in the UK like Clapton, Townshend, Hendrix and various Beatles and Stones frequented the same clubs in London and attended each other's recording sessions and concerts for example Hendrix's Royal Albert Hall gig was attended by the Beatles and his final gig in the UK was attended by Eric Clapton. The Buffalo Springfield had the Native American connection through the name and Neil Young's image on stage. It is possible that they would try and associate themselves with the Native American cause to show affinity with the lifestyle that was also being adopted by the Hippies and others. Buffalo Springfield recognized very early on that the Native American ethos was more harmonious with nature at a time when plastic coated consumerism was rampant in Western Culture. Whatever their motives, there is a tendency for 'progressive rock bands' at this time to sing songs against the establishment and move towards the left politically. Buffalo Springfield had sung protest songs already and opposition to the war was growing. As Barry Melton said; "the top bands continued to play benefits and as opposition to the war grew stronger, the music of the counter culture became more popular".

The support for the antiwar movement increased when atrocities like My Lai became public knowledge. After that event the mainstream voters began to question what was happening in South East Asia. Slotkin gives a good example of a protester handing out antiwar leaflets outside someone's office. The observer noticed that for several weeks the protester was ignored by the general public but after the My Lai incident people started to take them.[30] It was as if people trusted in the decisions of their government and war was war but even a staunch conservative could recognize that the murder of women and children by American troops was wrong. Some of those people who took the leaflets were inspired to attend the meetings and rallies against the war. Here they would be exposed to the music that was an integral part of the event. This is one of the fundamental ways that the sixties changed things in the society and for the individual. People were exposed to things and events that normally they would not have been associated with. This would in some cases broaden their outlook. Growing up working class in the UK at that time was pretty glum. They were not exposed to the cultural qualities of life that the children of middle class parents were. These children generally attended grammar schools where they were educated in the finer things in life with the possibility of going on to university. In 1960 working class children were educated to go in the army or work in shops and factories. This type of life at the beginning of the sixties was clearly illustrated in the film of the book 'Saturday Night and Sunday Morning.' Many kids left school at 15 and became factory fodder. As an alternative to a life in 'England's Dark Satanic Mills' in the mid-sixties things started to change. Some young working class teenagers took their lifestyle and personal values that had been drilled into them by parents and schools up to revision and started dropping out. The ones that joined bands and became good did so partly because they had been conditioned with a work ethic in their upbringing that applied to whatever trade they chose. Art colleges that had sprung up under the Labour government provided enlightenment and a way out for the lucky few who were fortunate enough to attend them.

The American version of this situation can be clearly seen in the film of the musical 'Hair'. This musical was a groundbreaking play that introduced the genre of 'Rock Musical'. The film opens where a young draftee says goodbye to his Dad and leaves his home on the farm. The film develops during his stopover in New York on his way to boot camp. He meets up with a group of Hippies most of them coming from middle class backgrounds. Through his association with them and participating in some of their actions or happenings he is forced to examine his motivations and question some of his beliefs. With the result that he chooses his sense of duty and his responsibility to the way of life he has been bought up to believe in. This was true of many Americans; they did not all question authority and burn their draft cards. The film showed the strong sense of solidarity and social commitment that existed among the youth at that time. The consequence of this commitment is that one of the hippies takes the place of the draftee and is shipped to Vietnam where he is killed. This symbolizes that their opposition to the war was not due to lack of courage to go and fight. It took courage and conviction to refuse to be drafted because you were breaking the law by going against the government. You risked going to prison or you became a fugitive fleeing the country you grew up in and leaving behind your family and friends. This was no easy choice to make. It is worth noting that countries like Sweden took in 'Draft Dodgers' on humanitarian grounds and because of the international political climate that was starting to oppose American involvement in the Vietnam. Hair was conceived by actors James Rado and Gerome Ragni who began writing the play in late 1964. They based the characters on themselves and actual people they had met on the street. To do this they grew their hair long and hung out on the street attending 'Be Ins'. In 1966 Ragni performed in Megan Terry's play Viet Rock in the Open Theater. This was about young men being deployed to Vietnam and some of the exercises were used in 'Hair'.[31] This is particularly relevant in view of the fact that the Vietnam War played such a big part in the daily life of average Americans. Through the media and military personal in uniform were common features in train stations and bus terminals as they travelled home on leave. The play was based on the social conditions in the United States at that time. They wanted to get the feeling of the energy on the street and reproduce it onstage. "It was very important historically, and if we hadn't written it, there'd not be any examples. You could read about it and see film clips, but you'd never experience it. We thought, 'This is[32] happening in the streets,' and we wanted to bring it to the stage." Theatre reviewer Scott Miller encompasses most of the elements in his review of 'Hair'.

"The youth of America, especially those on college campuses, started protesting all the things that they saw wrong with America: racism, environmental destruction, poverty, sexism and sexual repression, violence at home and the war in Vietnam, depersonalization from new technologies, and corruption in politics.... Contrary to popular opinion, the hippies had great respect for America and believed that they were the true patriots, the only ones who genuinely wanted to save our country and make it the best it could be once again.... [Long] hair was the hippies' flag – their... symbol not only of rebellion but also of new possibilities, a symbol of the rejection of discrimination and restrictive gender roles (a philosophy celebrated in the song "My Conviction"). It symbolized equality between men and women. In addition... the hippies' chosen clothing also made statements. Drab work clothes (jeans, work shirts, pea coats) were a rejection of materialism. Clothing from other cultures, particularly the Third World and Native Americans, represented their awareness of the global community and

their rejection of U.S. imperialism and selfishness. Simple cotton dresses and other natural fabrics were a rejection of synthetics, a return to natural things and simpler times. Some hippies wore old World War II or Civil War jackets as way of co-opting the symbols of war into their newfound philosophy of nonviolence"

The Hippies in 'Hair' might have been co-opting the military uniforms into their philosophy of no-violence but this was not the intention of Rock musicians also using the same military look. Bands like the Buffalo Springfield used whole civil war military uniforms together with guns in their promotional photo shots. They reached back into that period of history and re-enacted the characters from that time adapting images of young men that had served in another conflict. The Calvary trooper or Confederate officer together with the cowboy were the most favoured.

The Buffalo Springfield disbanded according to Neil Young "just before they broke up Buffalo Springfield were not improving". They might not have been improving but they were getting excellent reviews for their live performances during that period and Rolling Stone magazine deemed their last album as "the most beautiful record they've ever made." Bill Graham tried to persuade them to play a four night booking at the Fillmore and Ahmet Ertegün wanted them to go on a British tour with the Beach Boys.[33] They had always been stars in Los Angeles but they just could not achieve nationwide acclaim. So despite all the reviews and attempted persuasion the Buffalo Springfield 'threw in the towel' and after two and a half years they finally quit in May 1968. At a party at Cass Elliot's house Crosby Stills and Nash made an improvised presentation of some of their songs. After reputedly failing an audition with Apple Records Crosby, Stills and Nash released their first album in May 1969 on Atlantic under the auspices of Ahmet Ertegün. Who was described by Keith Richards: "as an 'Elegant Turk',[34] who drove the music business into a total re-think of what it was that people could hear. The echoes of the Stones idealism resonated. Ahmet encouraged talent. He was very much hands on. It was not like EMI or Decca, some huge conglomerate. That company (Atlantic) was born and built up out of love of music, not business." Ahmet had been an ardent believer in the potential of Buffalo Springfield. He continued to have faith in Stills by giving CSN a recording contract and it was his idea to incorporate Neil Young into the band. The first album 'Crosby, Stills and Nash', spawned two hit singles and when Neil Young joined in 1969 their next album 'Déjà vu' released in March 1970 became an instant bestseller and generated three hit singles. CSN&Y became the first Stadium Super group and were the only American band to rival the Beatles in social political influence. The time span between these events clearly shows how close Buffalo Springfield was to achieving success. Their subsequent best of album 'Retrospective' released in February 1969 went platinum.

EULOGY FOR BUFFALO SPRINGFIELD

Neil Young offers a fitting epitaph to the group's demise: "It was good, but we didn't know what we were doing so we didn't know how much fun we were having until it was all over. Everybody thought, "Wow that must have been a lot of fun." We were just there. I think the Springfield broke up at the right time. I don't think they were improving when they broke up."[35]

The Buffalo Springfield was not a temporary success act. They achieved some recognition and chart success during their two-year existence and have now been acknowledge as a major influence on American music during the sixties. All the members were highly talented musical artists. The three main songwriters in the group: Ritchie Furay, Stephen Stills and Neil Young went on to produce musical works of quality over the next five decades! Arguably the most successful was Neil Young who was always changing his style with the times and had his albums in the charts every decade since the breakup of Buffalo Springfield. He might not have achieved the commercial success levels his work reached in the sixties and seventies but he has always been an artistic presence that has inspired new bands and satisfied his traditional fans as well as attracting new fans from the younger generations that were not familiar with his early work. It is very important to note that although the story of Buffalo Springfield is marred by break-ups and disagreements it was not always like that. In the beginning, as we can see from the TV shows and personal recollections they had a great time and their records sales after they split up prove they made some really great music that would stay with fans and inspire bands to come. The chemistry between Young and Stills continued when they co-operated on projects during their subsequent musical careers. This is testimony to their friendship and skills as musicians and songwriters. For their image as a band in their early work they reached into the second half of 19th century, The Wild West. They could have done this for several reasons. Previously during the early sixties bands like Paul Reverie and the Raiders had donned uniforms of the American War of independence to symbolically repulse what was known as the British invasion lead by the Beatles. These stylish theatrical costumes were not suited for wearing offstage. When LA became the new music centre of America he casual Western look adapted by bands from there was well suited offstage to the local environment and the climate, sunshine, deserts, canyons and ranches. California had become the nucleus of Flower Power and the Hippy Movement that supplied the counter culture with an alternative outlook and music that was dominating the music charts and challenging the conventional rules in society. In another way by adopting the dress of the cowboy and outlaw they are identifying with the people who lived free and unharnessed lives as opposed to modern day technocrats who were shackled to the careers and as Dylan says "just saw themselves as something they invest in."[36] This music became the soundtrack of youth during the sixties and as I will later show it transcended boundaries between the establishment and what became known as the counter culture. Two of the seminal focal points musically in America in that decade were "The Monterey Music festival" which was the ground breaker showing that a festival of popular music could be accepted. It had never been done before and two of the people who had absolute faith in the idea were the organisers John Philips from the Mamas and the Papas and Beatle Paul McCartney. The next big event in the world of popular music was "Woodstock". Neil Young should have been at both events but he was only at the latter. Fourteen days before The Monterey Music festival he had one of his notorious leaving the band episodes and Stephen Stills had to press on with the engagement using friend David Crosby who was also appearing at the festival with the Byrds as a replacement for Neil Young. Wearing a tasselled jacket and Cowboy hat he looked the part. Crosby had always been a controversial figure and during the introduction of the Byrd's performing Bob Dylan's 'He was a friend of mine.' At Monterey Crosby lashed out about the supposed cover up in the JFK conspiracy theory. Telling people it was their country and they had a right to know the truth. This was not appreciated by the other Byrds who did not always shared Cosby's views. [37]

JAMES MAZZEO.

James Mazzeo [38] the Artist has known Neil Young from the early Buffalo Springfield days and is familiar to Neil Young fans as the designer of two of his albums 'Zuma' and 'Greendale'. Neil Young rates Greendale as something special that many fans seemed to have overlooked. Greendale appears in three forms as a book (illustrated by Mazzeo), record and film. James Mazzeo along with other Neil Young compatriots like the late great Ben Keith appears in the film Greendale. Some Rusties who have met Mazzeo have said that his life story is so interesting and relevant to the period it should be made into a movie. He was living in Haight Ashbury in the 1965-66 period right
when it was all happening. He started doing light shows at concerts in 1966. This makes him an excellent witness to the events that happened around then. I asked James Mazzeo in April 2009 for his impressions about Neil Young and his use of Native American Imagery and any other recollections that he might have. He gives some interesting details about a 'Brocken Arrow' sculpture he created in 1972.

Mazzeo -April 6, 2009: *"I've known Neil since my first light show gigs in 1966....he used to wear long fringed leather jackets and patched Levi pants....on the road we would stop and buy Indian blankets and stuff.....Neil likes Native American art and such but is not obsessed....he has a good eye for design and would rely on the graphic impact of native works to use with his writings and sometimes elements would be used in his stage settings. We lived together on his ranch and at the beach in Malibu in the 1970's and on his boat sailing the pacific....I never saw him in a loin cloth, body paint or sporting a bow and arrow or tomahawk......we captured many brains along the way but we never took a scalp"*.

I was referred to James Mazzeo by Rustie 'Joel' who told me James has been a friend of Neil's for over 30 years. I have quoted his messages in full because he is closely connected to Neil Young. As James did 'Light Shows' in 1966 he was very active on the LA scene in a creative capacity. He knew Neil from the Buffalo Springfield days and confirms here that Neil wore "Long Fringed Jackets." He points out that Neil likes Native American art and crafts but is not obsessed with it. He discusses how Neil uses the graphic impact of Native works in his writings and sometimes in his stage settings. After living with Neil on his ranch in the 1970's and knowing him personally. James is a very dependable primary source; obviously they go way back as mates and continue to be friends.

Mazzeo - April 17, 2009 ...." *his ranch is called BROKEN ARROW RANCH ... after the first song he wrote that brought in a million dollars when he was 21 years old. notice the broken arrow.....the image is inspired from Neil's song BIG TIME on his BROKEN ARROW album....here is a photo of the road on his ranch to his recording studio...I made him that giant BROKEN ARROW sculpture for his ranch in 1972 "* "*the sculpture originally hung from a big branch on a big fir tree by the studio but after 20 years it looked like the branch was gonna break so Neil designed the road arch ...it looks great like that!*"

Further correspondence with James Mazzeo resulted in some images of a giant Broken Arrow symbol be designed for Neil in 1972. He gives some information here about Neil buying the ranch with his first big royalty cheque for the song Broken Arrow.

There is some conflict here, according to several sources[39] Neil brought Broken Arrow in 1970 when he would have been 24. Neil wrote Broken Arrow in 1967 when he was 21 and it was on Buffalo Springfield Again. However, that album only sold 200,000 copies originally [40] and Neil Young says of Buffalo Springfield's finances: "*We always owed. We never got out of hock*"[41] I would purpose the royalties came from the Buffalo Springfield album Retrospective. Released in 1969 after the group had split up it went 'Gold' and eventually 'Platinum' in record sales? Neil's first big commercial success came in 1972 with Harvest which features songs like Old Man that were based on people who lived at the ranch. The back cover shows a picture of the band playing in his barn. Neil also mentions buying the ranch when talking in between songs at a concert. [42]

When he talks about the ranch foreman who asks: "*How did a young fellow like you get enough money to buy this place?*" to which Neil replies, "*I dunno just lucky I guess*" and the foreman replies "*That's the darndest thing I ever heard.*" This often happens when people recall from memory 'how it was' especially when 40 years have gone by. The information about the sculpture is valuable in that the original purpose was not to use it as a road arch and the fact it has been moved from the original place. The name Broken Arrow obviously means a lot to Neil as I have discussed already.

On the album he dedicates the song to Ken Koblun *"who loomed large in Springfield's history: some thought he was an Indian….explains Ken, because it's an Indian term for friendship after a war"*[43] Neil had had a dispute with Ken, the dedication was probably a sign of 'no hard feelings.'

Mazzeo, wrote, April 17, 2009: *"as far as I know….Neil never dressed 'completely' in Indian outfits….he did have many fringed jackets some with some beadwork…..he wore them before CSN&Y with the Buffalo Springfield…he had a special patched pair of faded worn levis that he only wore on stage for a number of years…but that was more hippy than Indian…I never saw him or a picture of him with a feather in his hair…he might have had a feather or two on his guitar strap but not regularly…..I was living in Haight Ashbury 1965-66 and lots of hippies were wearing Indian jewelleries and accessories….moccasins and such….Neil had a few pairs of beaded moccasins. he might have worn them for a photo session but not on a regular basis….he has used his Indian blankets to cover the seats of his 1948 Buick road master fastback….and more in his private coach which we call 'Pocahontas.'"*

Here James confirms that he had 'many' fringed jackets and some with beadwork. The patched Levis are probably the one use on the cover of "After the Gold Rush" and "Déjà vu" and James describes the style as more 'hippie' than Indian. James is an important source as he lived in Haight Ashbury, which at that time was right in the centre of where it was all happening.

TV documentaries from the sixties show bus tours taking tourists through Haight Ashbury so they can look at the Hippies. The term 'Freaks' and 'Freak Show' were not always complementary many mainstream Americans actually viewed the Hippies as Freaks (i.e. abnormal) Mazzeo confirms that in this period 'lots of hippies' were wearing Indian jewellery and accessories.

Neil uses Indian blankets in his cars and calls his coach 'Pocahontas.' This further reinforces the verbal connection between the name, Neil Young and Native American terms i.e. "Where is Neil? He has just left Broken Arrow driving Crazy Horse to LA in Pocahontas." James Mazzeo was very helpful in answering my mails and I am indebted to him for the information gathered here. An artist sometimes sees the past in a different light and his recollections of the period are very descriptive.

NEIL YOUNG ABANDONS THE HOLLYWOOD INDIAN IMAGE.

A more obscure abstract reason Neil Young used the Native American imagery is that it gave him confidence. It became his character onstage as a performer and the mask acted as a shield. Neil Young was not very sure of his voice in the beginning of his career and he did not sing. Perhaps taking on another persona helped him to overcome that.

He is a Canadian and because of the vast tracts of wilderness in that country and the symbol of the Maple leaf they are universally associated with the nature with its mountain ranges, forests and the people of the First Nations. This is the image Neil Young adopted.

This general image people have of Canada seems to naturally incorporate the people of the First Nations.

While in CSN&Y he says:

"When I was in the Springfield I held back" he goes on to say "I was paranoid about my voice. So on my own first LP I buried my voice intentionally. The second LP I bought it up more. I had more confidence. That's what working with Crazy Horse has done. It's given me confidence." [44]

As he evolves as a solo artist and becomes more self-confident he drops the Hollywood Indian role. Is this because he no longer needs the protective image of the Indian?

He still has a love of Native American Art and design, this is evident in his use of the images for his band and merchandise but on a personal level, he has moved away from it. Although he dropped the style he remains firmly in the historical period using the image of the riverboat gambler as seen on Déjà Vu and later he is often seen sporting Cowboy hats like in the movie 'Heart of Gold'. Another aspect could have been that he saw the role of Indian as his role in the band and when he went 'solo' he lost that association. This is the genius of calling the group by the member's surnames. They can remain individuals performing their own songs almost as solo artists being accompanied by the band. The photographs in the "Neil Young Songbooks" show clearly he did not promote the way of dressing as Hollywood Indian after he left Buffalo Springfield.

NEIL YOUNG JOINS CSN.

Musically Neil Young added the raw energy of his driving lead guitar to the 'CSN sound.' This complemented Stephen Stills guitar style and they continued playing 'guitar duels' like in the Springfield days. David Crosby is very close to Neil Young in image and style. Some of his songs 'Lee Shore' and 'Triad' have an affinity with Neil Young's style of song writing while 'Almost Cut My Hair and Wooden Ships' has some of the raw rock sound that Neil Young projects in his music. Neil told Crosby that 'Almost Cut My hair' was his favourite song on Déjà Vu. Both Crosby and Nash have co-operated with Neil Young on musical projects like 'Harvest' where they sing harmonies. Young has in turn appeared on some of their solo efforts, noticeably Crosby's 'If Only I Could Remember My Name', the song "Music is Love" is also included on 'Archives' Neil Young also bought his image or brand with him to CSN&Y as the dark sad loner clad in white frilled shirt and the western attire of a gambler or Outlaw. David Crosby seemed to adopt the old Neil Young look by wearing a tasselled jacket similar to the one Young wore in the Buffalo Springfield thereby maintaining and reinforcing the group's frontier image. He did this to such an extent that the journalist Greg Marcus reviewing CSN&Y Woodstock debut in Rolling Stone magazine states:

"David Crosby finally looks exactly like Buffalo Bill, his flowing hair and twisted moustache"[45] David Crosby incorporated a buckskin tasseled jacket into his stage persona at one of the creative heights in his career and can be seen on the cover of one of his best albums "If Only I could Remember My Name" one of the songs on that record 'Cowboy Movie' tells the story how CSN&Y came apart at the seams. Although Crosby's jacket is almost identical to the one worn by Neil Young, with his cowboy hats and moustache he takes on the image of a frontier scout and not a Native American. Neil Young very rarely wore the fringed jackets after he joined CSN&Y one exception was when they did a concert at the Big Sur in 1969.[46] Their interactions with each other's solo projects, (Neil Young often using aliases because of contractual restrictions) shows a lasting affinity between the members of CSN&Y that cumulated in 2008 when they reunited for the 'Freedom of Speech Tour' that was documented in the film Déjà vu. This tour was a vehicle for Neil Young to perform his "Living in War" album where he spoke out against President George W. Bush and the war in Iraq. Being over 60 Neil Young held back in voicing his opposition to the Gulf War. He was waiting for the younger generation to take up the flame and carry on the tradition of protest songs, when this did not happen he organized the Freedom of Speech tour with CSN.

MAKING THE COVER OF DÉJÀ VU 1970.

It is Crosby and not Neil Young who is wearing the tasseled jacket on the cover of the Déjà vu, album. He is adapting a classic frontier pose: sitting cradling a long hunting rifle similar to the type used by Buffalo Hunters in the post American civil war period. There is no mistaking the likeness between Crosby and Buffalo Bill in this picture. He bears a very strong moustache that always helped identifying the European settler from his Native American counterpart. Also missing in Crosby's attire are the Native American beads, chocker and Bear Claw necklaces that Neil Young sported in his Buffalo Springfield days. David Crosby seems to have replaced Neil Young, or at least the image that Young had in the Buffalo Springfield. In the early days Crosby did in fact substitute Young a few times, most noticeably at Monterey Pop Festival where he wore a tasseled jacket and Cowboy hat. It is possible that Stills used Crosby to fill a vacuum not just musically but also visually in the group's stage image. Crosby maintained the rugged 'Wild West' frontier dimension in the group's image that Neil Young had abandoned. Young was now developing the more sophisticated Western Dandy or gambler image. He wore frilled white shirts, three quarter length coats and his patched jeans. He maintained this image for his solo efforts as well as using it as his stage persona with the band. There was no radical difference in Neil Young's musical style at that time and musically he incorporated some of his solo efforts like 'Down by the River' and 'Southern Man' into the CSN&Y live performances.

On the cover of Déjà vu, Young is wearing a gun belt. It is not as visible because his hands are folded across the buckle. In another promotional photograph (from the same photo session) used by Atlantic to promote the album the gun belt is clearly visible and Young has his hand on the holster. The album was released in March 1970,[47] at the height of the Vietnam antiwar demonstrations. Young's song "Ohio" is based on the "Kent State Massacre" that first occurred two months later in May 1970 and therefore did not appear on Déjà vu. Had it occurred before the album was released because of sensitivities it is quite probable that the band would not have posed with guns on the cover. The song did appear on their next album, which was the double album "4 Way Street" by that time "Ohio" had become an anthem representing to millions of young people and student's across American a clear statement against this despicable act of aggression by the United States Government against unarmed students.

During the sixties there was a prominent affiliation with guns in American society especially noticeable through the daily media coverage of the war in Vietnam where young GI's were often bearing weapons. In the mid-sixties Spaghetti Westerns appeared portraying Cowboys in an attire of bandoliers and pistols. It was especially evident in adverts for music in magazines like Rolling Stone. A good example is the album cover to Country Joe and the Fish 'Feel Like I am Fixin to Die'.[48] Here Country Joe depicts a Mexican bandit with bandolier and Winchester, while Barry Melton poses in a quasi-uniform complete with Sam Brown belt and Stars and Stripes arm band. The rest of the band are dressed more conventionally as magicians and bassist Bruce Barthol appears to be dressed in a Gorilla suit, on the back he is spotting a Butch Cassidy style hat. There is no such combination of themes on the cover of Déjà vu. This album cover comes right out of the American frontier ca 1865. There is no evidence in this image to connect it to the present time. The band members pose with tasselled jackets Winchester rifles, gun belts, bandoleers and Confederate uniforms. The sepia toning gives it the appearance of a portrait from the idyllic Old West, faded by time. Archaic lettering similar to the style used to promote Wild West Show on posters during the 19th century. There are the names of all the band members including the unknown drummer Dallas Taylor and bassist Greg Reeves. The small touches like the dog standing in the center,[49] and an old style western guitar in front of Neil Young helps to create a feeling of authenticity. It is reminiscent of a picture taken of a gang of outlaws holed up somewhere. Note how the African American Greg Reeves who has Native American heritage,[50] stands a little to the back which is how a black man from that period would have naturally placed himself. This American album cover is artistically one of the most outstanding from the close of the decade. It is definitely an overlooked American heirloom from the sixties representing both Rock music and the Old West. The cover was created by the veteran rock photographer Tom Gundelfinger.[51] Tom had studied art at various American universities and a small school in Paris and it was here he acquired the fundamental basics of Art and design. He was not influenced by the psychedelic poster artists of the time. However he did experiment with hand paint on photographs and 'psychedelicized' a photo of the 'Mamas and Papas' that gained him access to take pictures at the Monterey Festival which was the launch pad for an eight year stint in LA as Rock photographer. He became a known creator of album covers who had access to the artists and preferred working one on one as opposed to shooting stage performances.

" I had no idea what I was in for. Stephen (Stills) told me they wanted it to look as authentic as possible with a sepia tone effect. So I found a civil war era camera, I was able to rent which was used as a prop for movies. I then began to investigate what it would be like to do the tin type process which was something like a type of photo made for the Civil War era. The more research I did, I realized how difficult it was going to be to get all the materials and chemical to make it work. I was in for a lot of work, I finally came up with a process that was representative of that era – a tin type process, however the contrast wasn't good enough for reproduction, so I ended up using another old process using a Talbot sun print process made from a master negative. The photo that was used for the colour *separation for the cover was actually a photo I made on a poster board. I coated the board with a homemade materials and taking the master negative which was put into a printing frame made the exposure into the sun, which was a practice used in 1845"*[52]

Tom's description of his work on the Déjà Vu album cover clearly reveals the craftsman's pride in producing a piece of work that comes as close to perfection as possible. Even to the extent of mixing old formulas of chemical solutions that were used at the time to reproduce the desired effect. On his website Tom gives a more formal description of the process, note how the dog became included in the shot:

"Stephen Stills requested that I use the same photo techniques from the civil war era. I loaded a Matthew Brady type 8x10 civil war era camera with a 5x7 tintype. The exposure was two and a half minutes long. During the exposure I backed up the shot with conventional black and white plus X film. During the long exposure the dog walked into the center of the group and spontaneously became part of the photograph. The tintype in the 8x10 camera was technically not suitable for reproduction for lack of contrast. Therefore, I used a 35mm negative and made a 8x10 inter-negative which I contact printed to a special fiber board coated with chemicals; a Fox Talbot technique from the 1850's. This image was exposed in the sun, and is known as a sun print. The goal of this process was to replicate in its purest form, the original photographic process of the civil war era." [53]

The layout of the original album covers also has an attention to detail that was lost on some of the later reissues. The refinement of the originals released in 1970 can be seen in the thick texture of the black patterned cardboard used and the gold leaf lettering for the title. The actual picture pasted onto the gatefold sleeve, the corners have been cropped to give the effect of a photograph mounted on the page. This was a technique used in old photo albums before photo corners where there were four slits cut into the page and the corners of the photo was mounted in them. More pictures of the band are displayed inside the gatefold sleeve, most notably two of David Crosby in his beaded Native American jacket. In one of the shots Crosby gives the peace sign, Greg Reeves appears wearing a Cowboy hat similar to the one he is wearing on the cover. I have found four pictures from the cover of Déjà vu photo session. I describe the clothes in detail on the last picture, as it is lighter and easier to see. As it was standard to take more than one film in those days it is quite possible that more than these four exist.

The second picture from the same photo session was used by Atlantic for a full page advertisement in Rolling Stone Magazine,[54] reveals an even bolder Wild West sentiment. There is no dog in this picture and David Crosby is sitting on the branch behind Neil Young with his legs stretched out. Here Greg Reeves is seated holding a rifle and his holster is clearly visible. Even more striking in this picture Crosby, Nash and Greg Reeves are all wearing

Cowboy hats. Neil Young's gun belt which is hidden by his hands on the album cover is clearly visible and his right hand is resting on the holster. The rifle held by Dallas Taylor is in profile clearly showing it is a Winchester model, which is not clear on the album cover because of the angle.

The third picture from the Déjà vu photo session can be seen in Neil Young's second songbook (the one with the picture from the inner sleeve of the album 'After the Gold Rush' on the cover) this shot is lighter and the clothes more distinguishable. Greg Reeves the bass player looks solemn. He is wearing an ethnic style vest with a large flower on each side and his bone handled colt six-shooter is clearly visible in the holster. Next to him but standing a little back is Stephen Stills. This positioning would not be appropriate for the period it is trying to depict. The shot used for the cover where Greg Reeves stands to the rear is more realistic. Stephen Stills looks solemn with his hand resting by the side of his saber. He is dressed in a high waist Confederate jacket from the American Civil War. Neil Young is sitting down and looks happy. He is wearing a white shirt with frills down the front and a three quarter length black coat. He is wearing his cherished patched jeans that he also wears on the cover of the After the Gold Rush album. You can clearly see the gun and holster. Graham Nash is dressed like one of the US miners from 1849 or a railroad navvy. He is standing smoking what looks like an old style clay pipe. He looks serious and is the only one without a weapon. Not bearing arms could allude to the fact he is English and does not have the same cultural background as the others. At the time England was renowned throughout the world for not having an armed police force; enough said 'Bless its Little Pointed Head'. David Crosby is sitting down, smiling and dressed in the tasseled jacket that he often wore during that period. He is holding a Winchester rifle. The butt of the rifle is on his knee and the barrel is pointing up, he has his finger on the trigger and three fingers in the reload bracket. Dallas Taylor looks very solemn. He is dressed in a high waist embroidered Comanchero jacket. The style worn by the Mexican cowboys that traded with the Comanche Indians.[55] There is a bandoleer over his shoulder with bullets in it. He is wearing jeans and holding a Winchester rifle by the top of the barrel with the butt on the ground.

The fourth picture can be seen on Tom O'Neal's website,[56] along with three similar outtakes plus one of the group from the side. Tom also took the picture of David Crosby in a tasseled jacket from 1969 that was used on his 3 CD box collection "Voyage,"[57] Crosby is wearing the same jacket at the Big Sur concert from 1969 that can be seen on YouTube. In some of other pictures in Tom's collection Crosby is sporting a furry hat which is similar to the one that he wore with the Byrd's and those used by Kiowa Native Americans.

THE RELATIONSHIP BETWEEN NEIL YOUNG AND STEPHEN STILLS.

Neil Young said of Stephen Stills "he is like a brother to me, I have known longer than anyone else I know". Much like brothers there was sometimes a lot of friction between their personalities. These differences contributed to the breakup of Buffalo Springfield. Regardless of these fallouts, they have always found each other again. Their music styles and personalities are very different but have many common denominators. They can both sing and perform solo on Western acoustic guitars. This is part of their heritage from 'back in the old folky days.' They became very infamous for their long electric guitar duals while playing together.[58] They both played with Jimi Hendrix on a number of occasions and he gave them both inspiration and some pointers about electric guitar playing. Young credits Hendrix as an inspiration in a song,[59] and Hendrix played on the solo album 'Stephen Stills'. Hendrix contributed so much to music in the 60's. Through his innovative guitar playing he became ingrained in the soundtrack of that period. For that generation he is right up there with the Beatles as a major contributor. Neil Young and Stephen Stills were both very much children of their time, they had met only once before they formed Buffalo Springfield together. This was while Stills was touring in Canada and the event is mentioned in the song 'Long May You Run,' where Neil sings: "Back in Blind River in 1962, when I last saw you alive". As Stephen Stills says when they met they behaved like ordinary teenagers who hung out together and became friends, absorbing the atmosphere of change going on around them, playing music and drinking beer. A lot of things were happening at that time in the US due to the British invasion. To be doing what they were doing in the mid-sixties was not a secure career path. They must have felt united as 'kindred spirits' because Stills had tried to contact Young in Canada several times, only to learn Young had broken up the band and embarked on a solo career. Young had tried to find Stills by going to New York where he met Ritchie Furay who told him Stills had moved to LA. With his career going nowhere after "The Mynah Birds" dissolved Young makes a last ditch attempt to find Stills by driving to LA in his Hearst. There was tenacity in this story that shows somehow 'this was meant to happen.' When Buffalo Springfield formed, they were both accomplished musicians who were searching for some way to succeed and break into the music business. Their main goal was to be stars. Neither of them knew Dewey Martin who was bought in to play drums. Young and Bruce Palmer had been playing together in a band. The same applied to Stills and Ritchie Furay. The five of them had only rehearsed for a week before they started touring with the Byrds. That is not really much time to become acquainted with each other let alone form a band.

Stills is often depicted as the pushy one who led the band and made the connections and contacts that helped the Buffalo Springfield break into the music business. He did write their first hit 'For what it's Worth 'and is listed on the back of the first album as being the leader "but we all are." He was slightly unscrupulous in his approach to forming the band for example he convinced Ritchie Furay to leave his secure job and come to LA to join a band that at the time only existed in Still's head. Whatever the beginnings as the band developed the strong individual talents of the members started to emerge and they started to pull in different directions. This is fine for a band that is established or only has one or two creative sources directing it. But it is difficult for a group that only has one week's rehearsal as ballast. Compare that to the foundation of other bands like the Beatles or Stones who grew up together in their respective towns.[60] The members of the Buffalo Springfield did not even come from the same country let alone the same town. This singer songwriter combination and the fact that with Furay there were three lead singers is what made Buffalo Springfield so unique and gave the band an edge over other more harmonious groups that did not suffer from these internal conflicts. One has to say that they do appear to be having a good time when you look at their promotional photo shots and TV shows where they are often seen fooling around. [61]

Stills played the Cowboy while Young played his antithesis the Indian. Later on they continued to represent opposites, Stills portraying slick image of the Steamboat South while Young was the epitome of the kind of people wandering around the blue rugged Canadian Rockies. It was 19th century Confederate culture contra the hobo ethics of the Mountain man. That is how they appeared in the band. Neil always tried to depict the outsider, the guy on the 'losing end' who still managed to remain center stage. Neil Young by his temperament seems to identify with the underdog who might have lost but was never a weakling: The Comanche Warrior was held in high esteem during the war on the plains just as the Confederate Calvary was a tough adversary respected by the Northern Troops.

Stephen Stills likes to associate with the Southern gent or the slick cowboy. His songs were upbeat like "Dusty Roads" that could almost be a poke at Young: "I don't tell no tales about no hot dusty roads. I am a city boy and I stay at home. I make no excuses I just don't want to roam and I don't like being alone"[62] On his first solo album Neil Young airs a similar sentiment in the song called "The Loner" which was reputed to be about Stills: "He's a perfect stranger, like a cross of himself and a fox. He's a feeling arranger and a changer of the ways he talks. He's the unforeseen danger the keeper of the key to the locks. Know when you see him, nothing can free him. Step aside, open wide, it's the loner". Then on a more personal note he talks about a love lost that many people interpret as a reference to Still's relationship to the singer Judy Collins. Another Lady of the Canyon who had a major hit with the Joni Mitchell song 'Both Sides Now' and the traditional song 'Amazing Grace'. Young seems to insinuate here that something really died in Stills when he lost this love and nothing would free him from the torment: "There was a woman he knew, about a year or so ago. She had something that he needed and he pleaded with her not to go. On the day that she left, He died, but it did not show. Know when you see him, nothing can free him. Step aside, open wide, It's the loner." It is hardly complementary and could have been interpreted by Stills as being offensive. He knew the song was about him and to illustrate their camaraderie he did a version of "the Loner" on one of his solo albums called 'Illegal Stills'.[63] They knew that by playing together they could achieve their goals and that is what they did. Neil Young is notorious for leaving all the bands he has been in with Stephen Stills. Despite these setbacks Stills has always incorporated Young's vital ingredient to the music if he could see it would create the sound he wanted to achieve. Over the last four decades, they have collaborated on many projects. There is a unique chemistry between these two artists and whenever they collaborate some of the magic is captured on the tracks. There is a definite instability when Young is involved that does not occur when Stills is working together with Crosby and Nash. Likewise this instability does not happen when Young is working with Crazy Horse. In his collaborations with Stills, Young has always put the music first, as he says "he always follows his muse."[64] Neil Young has remained loyal to Stephen Stills and many of his old associates throughout his career. They sometimes re-appear with him during his tours for example when Bruce Palmer played with him during his 'Trans' tour in 1982. Young has played together with many fine outstanding musicians and created some of the most memorable music in the history of rock. Some of the finest moments have been created with Stills. What makes 'The Loner' such a great song is that Young might be writing about Stills but the image of the loner is such an integral part of the American identity. It has cultural connotations that can be seen for example in the Westerns of Bud Boetticher that were made during the late fifties and early sixties. Here he uses Randolph Scott as the loner who rides into every film alone at the beginning and almost always rides out alone in the end. Martin Scorsese and Clint Eastwood are both ardent Boetticher fans and Scorsese says in one of the film commentaries to the aptly named 'Ride Lonesome.' [65] "This image of the loner is something that the American audience can identify with and I have used it in my own films like 'Taxi Driver' ". Scorsese points out it was how the nation was built people solved their problems alone. In the same commentary Eastwood talks about 'the code' in cowboy films where there was a clear line between right and wrong what a man does and does not do. Even the villains seem to follow this code and Boetticher always gives them an affable dimension. We can relate to where they are coming from and through their actions they gain our sympathy and we want them to get a break. For these reason icons like Billy the Kid and Jesse and Frank James are endeared to Americans through folklore. They represent the oppressed who rose against the tyranny and fought the system. Therefore Country Rock bands could safely adopt the image of the outlaw without being derided because it is generally excepted that outlaws did what they did out of necessity or they were driven to a life of crime by some form of injustice. In many cases the image of the outlaw was more acceptable to Middle America than the image of the long haired peace loving hippie.

GUNS

There is a distinct paradox in the use of guns in the image of the country rock bands during the sixties. They have become associated with the counter culture through their music. At the same time they want to incorporate the image of the Wild West where guns played a major role, into the Country Rock image. In 1970 America was engulfed in violence internally with demonstrations and externally with the Vietnam War. CSN&Y's audience was made up of the generation that advocated the peace and love values of Woodstock. The group CSN&Y made their debut at Woodstock. The documentary film of the event "Woodstock" uses two of CSN&Y studio tracks in the introduction scenes. On promotional shots used by Atlantic to promote the album Déjà Vu the weapons are very clear. They are toned down for the actual album photo cover. This could reflect that they did not wish to have too much emphasis on the guns. Crosby's rifle is acceptable because it is an antique looking stage prop. Whereas Young's sidearm is too contemporary resembling the ones used by the police in the US. Guns are recurrent as a theme in connection with Neil Young during that period. On the inside of the gatefold sleeve of 'Everybody Knows this is Nowhere' his producer David Briggs poses with a Winchester rifle. In the US in 1969-70 there was an escalation in bands using guns as props their advertising. This was evident in music magazines and on LP covers. At this time there was a new wave of Westerns promoting the anti-hero.[66] It is possible that these films contributed towards making the Outlaw image fashionable as it became immensely popular during the sixties. There were posters everywhere showing Clint Eastwood the unshaven cigar chewing gunslinger. This image complemented the one used by country rock artists. Guns were everywhere in the society that in turn had become more violent due in part to the Vietnam War where guns and weaponry were shown daily in newsreels. The Black Panthers and the Weathermen had shown that the civil rights movements and antiestablishment groups were willing to resort to violent means to achieve their aims. Later in 1973, Indian activists from AIM used force in the siege at Wounded Knee on the Pine Ridge reservation where two activists were shot dead by heavily armed government forces. The media flashed photographs round the world of young Indian warriors holding rifles in the air in the traditional sign of victory. It is relevant to consider what messages these images were sending. On the one hand you have pictures of real Indian activists waving real guns and getting killed. On the other hand you have country rock bands evoking the same image in a stage act. In the case of the Cowboy the macho element also needs to be considered. The world of the cowboy is basically a male domain and part of a cultural heritage that is sometimes used in arguments justifying for the liberal gun laws. The solution in the Old West was to take the law into your own hands to achieve justice if necessary. Many of the western TV shows have a core theme of hitherto peaceful townspeople driven to take (usually violent) action in the face of some adversity like raiding Indians or bandits. Self-reliance 'Have Gun Will Travel' attitude always seems to win the day with no repercussions for the participants. A lot of young men in the western industrial nations grew up with these TV shows and images. They became a rite of passage especially for many youths growing up in America and to some extent the UK where the most popular films were Westerns and films about the Second World War. The latter put emphasis on whole populations interacting with a major conflict that involved the whole world whereas Westerns emphasized the role of the individual in the developments centered on an aspiring nation. In his biography Ringo Starr fondly remembers how many of the bands in the area of Liverpool adopted Western names. He also stated that you were never let down by Burt Lancaster when he starred in a Western.

NEIL YOUNG'S POLITICS.

Neil Young is no pacifist he believes in a military strong America if she is going to remain the guardian of freedom that she was through two world wars. But Young holds the politicians accountable for their actions concerning involvement in war and the legitimacy of committing the country to war. He supported Ronald Regan's unpopular policies of making sure America stayed a strong military power. But he did not support Bush's actions of starting the Iraq war and released the protest CD 'Living in War' in 2006 reflecting the political turmoil in the US and directly attacking Bush with one of the songs "Lets Impeach the President". He took the message on the road with the 'Freedom of Speech Tour'. Crosby, Still, Nash and Young have all contributed to each other's solo work and he recruited them to do the "Freedom of Speech Tour" voicing their opposition to President Bush's polices in the Middle East and what they saw as infringement of basic human rights of American citizens. This was made into an award winning film by Neil Young. In the film Stephen Stills can be seen working politically to support the Democrats and more recently Graham Nash was very visible during Barak Obama's campaign and he can be seen among the selected audience at President Obama's inauguration. These guys were no strangers to voicing their political opinions. They held back hoping that someone younger would take on the job and act as spokes person for their generation. Neil Young said he was waiting for someone younger to come along and write it but no-one did so when he turned 60 he did it himself. This again reflects the political consistency of the man, back in 1968 Buffalo Springfield made a political statement with 'For what it's Worth' criticizing police brutality. This song became an anthem of the 1960´s and is representative as a 'zeitgeist' that reflects the feeling of the decade. Young wrote 'Ohio' as a protest to the Kent State killings of four students and 'War Song' against the War in Vietnam. Finally 'Living in War' in 2006 against the War in Iraq and as the film shows they had positive and negative response but as Neil said: "we got a response, people got emotional about it and that's what I am trying to achieve", [67]

Even if he is not in favour of a war he does not take umbrage against the individuals who are sent to fight the war , they are soldiers doing their job. This is evident through various scenes of him interacting with veterans for example there is a scene in a documentary where he is introduced to his ranch foreman's nephew who is just back from a tour of duty in Vietnam. Neil Young warmly shakes his hand,[68] at a time when returning soldiers were being greeted by crowds chanting "Baby killers."[69] Neil Young can also be seen embracing Vietnam Vets during the Freedom of Speech tour in 2008. Many of them are now activists against George W. Bush and the war in Iraq.[70] This CD and tour is evidence that Neil Young's political involvement that started in the sixties and early seventies continues to this day. This personal commitment could be part of his popularity and loyal fan base. Native Americans have always honoured men who served in the armed forces regardless of politics.[71] We don't know if Neil Young consciously shares these values but he seems to emulate them. His Native American image is still resurrected regularly in magazine interviews and articles made long after Neil Young stopped using Comanche war jackets.

The Beat poets were very political and immensely influential; it is highly likely that people like Neil Young were drawn to Snyder's work. Much of Snyder's ethos about the environment appears to run parallel to Neil Young's. I have no evidence of this for the 1960s but in 1977 Snyder released a collection of work called "The Old ways" and in 1985 Neil Young released an album called "Old ways". It is difficult to know how common certain phrases are on different side of the Atlantic. "Ticket to Ride" for example sounds very original and exotic to English ears but Americans see it written over ticket booths in every train station. "Old Ways" could be coincidence but there is no doubt that the environment is big issue that they both have high on their agendas. Neil has organized "Farm Aid" concerts with other celebrities like Willie Nelson to support the cause of American farmers. This is in the same spirit as Gary Snyder who reads his poetry and lobbies for environmental causes during public appearances. As people they both appear to be drawn to the same sort of surroundings, mountains and forests. The worship of the nature as one of the Rusties put it "the forest is Neil's temple". To further, illustrate this affinity with nature. Neil Young was at one time looking to buy property in the same area where Snyder lives. This love of nature motivated many sixties artists to move to Laurel Canyon to absorbing the harmony of the nature. Joni Mitchell one of Neil's contemporaries wrote "Ladies of the Canyon" and John Mayall´s Blues breakers released "Blues from Laurel Canyon". This is one of the most fundamental factors of the sixties and vital in connection with understanding Neil Young, folk rock, country rock, The Byrds, Bob Dylan, The Band, Crosby Stills Nash, Crazy Horse they lived a lifestyle reflected in their music. Most of them rejected Hollywood mansions to live on ranches and in cabins. The clothes they wore onstage from the "Wild West" period of American History were also their clothes for everyday use. At that time in America people wore suits and ties to work. Singers like Dean Martin would wear a Tuxedo on stage. He might have sung songs like "Don't Fence Me In" with emotion but the last place he wanted to live was out on the prairie. In contrast, when Neil Young sang, "Home on the Range" he has a physical connection to the song as he raises a herd of Buffalo on his ranch.[72] His fans appreciate that and it sets him apart from the city slickers who sing about the country life but don't live it. Make no mistake about it when it comes to living in the country 'Neil is the real deal'

NEIL YOUNG, PROTEST SONGS

Neil young was involved in protest songs right from the early days when his band mate Stephen Still's penned the single **'For what it's Worth'** that appeared on Buffalo Springfield's first album in 1966. He has always written songs to protest about the situation in America and her involvement in what he saw as unjustified wars. Two years after 'Ohio' Neil Young wrote a protest song about what was going on in Vietnam, "War Song". He recorded the song with Graham Nash and released it as a single which through media coverage gave the antiwar movement even more support. I read about the single being issued solely in the US because Neil saw it as a domestic problem. So it was not officially issued in Europe. This was before the days of internet and instant access and it did not seem to get any airplay on the radio over here. I was fortunate enough to pick up a copy while I was on the road in 1972 travelling through Italy where they seemed to have a more lax attitude to those kinds of restrictions. **'War Song' 1972 Reprise Records, Neil Young and Graham Nash.** "They shot George Wallace down. He'll never walk around Mines are sleeping in the sea. Blow those bridges down Burn that jungle down and kill those Vietnamese."

The aggressive intensity of the lyrics are delivered with an abrasive rocking guitar rhythm. This was the year where the media coverage showing the horror of the war intensified, for example the classic photo of the naked child a girl running screaming burned by napalm. Life Magazine January issue listed the week's dead in Vietnam. The cover showed a young soldier smiling next to the American flag under the heading 'The One Boy Who Died'. People were speaking out and characteristically Neil Young went straight for the throat; 'Blow the bridges, burn the jungle, kill the Vietnamese' there is no mistaking the sentiment. He includes the political climate at home by including George Wallace the self-styled white hope of racists in the South.[73] Wallace was an unsavory character who condoned violent attacks on peaceful African American protesters using State troopers and police in the sixties.[74] By bringing into a song about shootings in the jungle the political incident where George Wallace was shot in 1972, Young shows that the methods used in the jungle have reached home turf and through incidents like this and Wallace's way of treating protesters "Wallace politics in the South were starting to mirror those in Saigon".[75] In another verse you have the daily life routine of waking up mixed with the sound of planes dropping mass destruction; 'In the morning, when you wake up, you got planes flying in your skies, their flying bombs, made to break up other lies in your eyes.' One of the familiar sounds of the Vietnam war was the hum of helicopters and the swoosh of jets flying low overhead. These were bought home to people through the media and became standard components in any film about Vietnam, notably the scene in 'Deer Hunter' that opens in Vietnam with the choppers coming in. All this was ingrained deep into the American psyche during the 60's and early 70's and all the soldiers who served in Nam were bonded by this experience in a very profound way. The young people who protested against the war were united in their cause and when the war was over they could resume normal life. But for many young soldiers barely out of their teens returning to normal life and trying to blend in again became a life long ordeal. **'Ohio' 1970 Atlantic Records, Crosby, Stills, Nash and Young.** 'Ohio' is CSN&Y's tour de force, Neil Young hated the War in Vietnam and he hated Nixon. At the Rainbow Concert in 1973, Young said, "Nixon likes me, says I'm good for the economy. I don't like him though, because of the four dead in Ohio." [76] Young wrote in the liner notes to the album Decade "It's still hard to believe I had to write this song. It's ironic that I capitalized on the death of these American students. Probably the most important lesson ever learned at an American place of learning. David Crosby cried after this take."

"Tin soldiers and Nixon coming / we're finally on our own / this summer I hear the drumming / four dead in Ohio. Gotta get down to it, Soldiers are gunning us down, should have been done long ago. What if you knew her then found her dead on the ground, how can you run when you know?" Crosby had showed him the newspaper with the image of the 14 year old runaway Mary Vecchio, on her knees with outstretched arms beside the body of one of the dead students.[77] Neil was clearly moved by the image he just knelt down on the floor in front of me and started writing the song with his guitar on his knees: "Tin soldiers and Nixon coming, we're finally on our own. This summer I hear the drumming, four dead in Ohio."

Here the words give you the fairy tale image of Tin soldiers. This cannot be happening in reality. The use of the word "drumming" to communicate the message associates with Native Americans. You can hear the drumming in the distance, what does it say? "Four dead in Ohio, Four dead in Ohio" This is ethnic, tribal, sending out the message by drum beat and the chanting the refrain: "Four dead in Ohio, Four dead in Ohio" Followed by the verse: "Gotta get down to it, Soldiers are gunning us down, Should have been done long ago. What if you knew her, and found her dead on the ground, how can you run when you know?" Here he personalizes the situation "What if you knew her and found her dead on the ground". It is the code right and wrong and you cannot distance yourself from the act because you know this girl. "How can you run when you know?" You can't you "Gotta get down to it" meaning get involved take a stance. The rough deep opening guitar riff is followed by almost shouted aggressive vocals. The song ends with the chanting finale, "four dead in Ohio", four dead in Ohio" and Crosby shouting over the top (ad lib) "Why? Why? How many more?" This was entertainment with a political message and as David Crosby later stated "It took a lot of guts back then to criticize Nixon like that but Neil got up on stage night after night and did it, he never faltered."

Neil Young gives an acoustic solo performance of this song on the 'Massey Hall' CD that shows the versatility of his songs. Another example of this versatility is the song 'On the Way Home' that is recorded with orchestra on Buffalo Springfield's album 'Last Time Around'. Neil gives an acoustic rendition on the CSN&Y live album '4 Way Street' this is many years before the popular tradition of 'unplugged'. I have tried to illustrate here how Neil Young was a very progressive musical artist pioneering new techniques and using expressions in his songs that we can all identify with. Especially for young people at that time there is no mistaking the message of 'Ohio'; "stand up and be counted". Leone Keegan was an 18 year old freshman at Kent State University she woke up to the sound of gunfire on campus as it happened. She wrote; "About a month after the shooting-I think it was June-Crosby, Stills and Nash, and Young gave an outdoor concert in Cleveland. It was the first time they'd sung that song "Ohio" live, and it was chilling. People were on their feet, you know, clapping their hands, moving their bodies crying. Everybody was just sort of shaking...You listen to the music now and it seems so candyish...then, it seemed to have a purpose. I'll never forget that night...(sings softly.) "....this summer I hear the drumming, four dead in Ohio...." [78] This description shows how emotionally moved the audience were by this song, it was chilling and the people were crying. Although she now finds it "candyish" she says she will never forget that night and softly sings the refrain from the song at the end of the interview. Ohio has become a part of the seventies anti-war protest soundtrack. The students were exercising their democratic right protesting against Nixon's escalation of the Vietnam conflict by attacking Cambodia. For all the people who heard it back then it will always be a document, a musical timepiece recording the event. For the individuals who were alive then it places a marker in their consciousness that they can associate with that period in their lives. The words of the song become a memorial that everyone can recall forty years after the tragic event. In this way Neil Young appealed to many young people through his music that were not necessarily part of the counter culture. As one student remembers on the 'song facts website': "With his words and music in songs like 'Ohio' he was saying something everyone could recognize and identify with. Kent State completely revolutionized my thinking and convinced me that the attitude of my forebears (right wing on steroids, you might say) was completely wrong. Whatever was going on, anywhere in the world, these murders were not justified. It was common to hear adults -- ordinary men and women -- state that the four deserved to die (should have been done long ago). Crosby was not wrong in his fear that those who denounced the government would be killed. I myself heard men say that this incident amounted to open season on "longhairs" and "radicals" -- cheerfully talking about killing their own sons and daughters if they expressed similar views or clothing-hair styles. Truly, it was an insane time. God bless Neil Young for his courage in speaking out then and now".[79] There were also the young people drafted into the military who tried to maintain some connection to normality by taking their music with them they could maintain part of their personal identity while have to go through a system that was specifically designed to dehumanize them. As Neil Young states in the film 'Déjà Vu' about the Freedom of Speech tour. "The draft united the young people at that time because it was effecting everyone" This could be part of the explanation that there is not the engagement against the Iraq war today that there was against Vietnam."[80] In another interview from 1988 that is shown in the same film Neil Young is wearing a Native American headband and he discusses how he looks upon the sixties and seventies:

"We were affected about what was going on and we wrote those songs. People reacted to the songs and that affected us. We were just there, we were part of the whole thing. I still think music is about feelings and whatever you feel if it happens to be political that is OK. But I don't think music should be totally designed to be a political thing."[81]

Here Young explains how the artist processes the things going on around him and creates something we can all recognize. Then it is up to people's personal taste if they like what is created or not. The facts speak for themselves that a lot people liked what CSN&Y were doing. For the artist and writer all forms of human condition can be categorized to some extent. As Thomas man wrote "When a young man sits down to write about his time, he writes about all young men from all times". There is a universal connection that young people have concerning common hopes and aspirations that all young people have that John F. Kennedy for example was so good at interpreting. "We all breathe the same air, we are all concerned about our children's future."

However there were limits in 1969 to what you had access to as Vietnam Vet Mike Cerre who was in Denang at that time explains; "CSN&Y were never politically correct enough to play on a USO tour so I never saw them in the seventies." Nevertheless he and other military personal did listen to the same music people were hearing in the States through the American Forces Network (AFN). He goes on to say: "I was a Marine Corps observer in Vietnam flying OB10 'Bronco's'. I remember flying back after missions, we used to tune in our planes high frequency radios and listen to Rock Music and their anthems just like the rest of my generation".

There is a school of thought that says the America could have won the war had it not been for all the public debate and political interference. This is also possible as it has since come to light that the North Vietnamese were at some stages ready to give up but all the turmoil on the US home front inspired them to carry on. There is no easy explanation for the whole Vietnam dimension on the American consciousness. The war went on for over 10 years and towards the end the media was dominated by pictures of wounded GIs and helpless civilians with crying children being carpet bombed by high altitude bombers. The jungle around their villages scorched with napalm and Agent Orange. For all concerned it was a good thing that the war ended sooner than later.

HIPPIE SONG

The song, 'Roll Another Number': from the album 'Tonight's the Night'. 1975. "I'm not goin' back to Woodstock for a while. Though I long to see that lonesome Hippie smile. I'm a million miles away from that helicopter day. No, I don't believe I'll be goin' back that way." Here Young sings about himself abandoning the Hippie values. He acknowledges that he will miss them, "Though I long to see that lonesome Hippie smile." The contradiction of Woodstock as an ethnic event: Helicopters and film crews. At the time Young was not happy with all the filming going on. For him that was not what music should be about and he refused to be filmed. Finally in the song he assures us he won't be going back that way. 'Roll another Number' was first performed on tour in 1973,[82] it signalled the passing of an era, the sixties were closing down. When he performed the song, Young told the audience "it was inspired by a journey along the Navajo Trail."[83] If you take the verse from 'Ambulance Blues' as an allegory of the closing of the sixties. The Navajo trail is an old Indian sheepherding trail going through Bryce Canyon, Arizona. It is breathtakingly beautiful; the first Anglo to cross it was John D. Lee in 1871. Symbolically 100 years before the sixties ended. This gives an impression of how 'new' the history of the 'Old West' really is and how the old converges with the new. "All along the Navajo Trail. Burn-outs stub their toes on garbage pails. Waitresses are cryin' in the rain, Will their boyfriends pass this way again?" This verse from 'Ambulance Blues', released in 1974. Here you get the feeling that the sixties really are over. When Neil performed 'Roll another Number' the year before this he was already starting to lose money on his tours and was sometimes having to pay the band out of his own pocket.[84] The Hippie ideal and other aspects like the Rock scene existed during the sixties, among other factors due to economic prosperity. When the sixties ended, music took on a more narrowly defined cultural role.[85] It took Neil longer to abandon the Long hair and Hippie dress style. Neil Young stated in an interview that he watched westerns on TV as a child. He might have got inspiration from this albeit subconsciously perhaps from a film like 'All along the Navajo Trail' (1945) a 'Music Western' starring Roy Rogers and Trigger. Many of the old Westerns from the late forties and fifties had songs and singing in them. This film was based on the book 'Sleepy Horse Range'[86] and includes the cowboy ballad 'Along the Navajo Trail,' "Well watta, ya know, it's mornin' already. There's the dawin' so silver and pale. It's time to clim into my saddle. And ride the Navajo trail."[87] It is possible that Young had seen the film 'All along the Navajo Trail' or heard the song as a child.

The lyrics to this song are in the style of 'a life on the open range' indeed Young did a cover of the song "Home on the range" for the soundtrack of 'Where the Buffalo Roam' an early version of 'Fear and Loathing'. 'Sleepy Horse Range' could easily pass for a Neil Young song title. It is reminiscent of the Neil Young carbon copy by the band America called 'A Horse with no Name.' This song was so close to Neil Young's style that people mistook it for him. Neil Young is firmly embedded in Country and Western music. He identifies with it as an artist and adopted the Western image at various stages during his career. In 1984 he played at 'The Grand Old Oprey'[88] and toured extensively in the South seeking acceptance and approval in his new role as a country artist. It was retracing his steps back to country rock and 'going to the country' by taking the rock out. This style is repeated in the film 'Heart of Gold' released in 2006. In the eighties Neil Young started supporting Ronald Regan and was criticized for having right wing sympathies.[89] Neil Young justifies this in his belief that only a strong America will be able to confront threats to the Western lifestyle. Anyone supporting Regan at that time was considered ultra conservative and possibly 'Redneck' a label that does not really fit Neil Young's image. Young's image has become more associated with the South and Southern outlook. This is partly due to his country style and his song themes. Both Dylan and Neil Young worked in Nashville at various stages in their career. Along with giving them the status of regular hard working musicians, the atmosphere in the recording studio was reputed to be more relaxed and the session musicians 'top notch'. Young appeared on the prestigious Johnny Cash show gaining more mainstream acceptance, the country music market being a considerable one with a long heratige that inspired many of the sixties rock bands like the Beatles and the Stones.

RECORDS AS PRIMARY SOURCES.

In the sixties records were made of vinyl and came in different categories:

Single, Sometimes called a 45 because it played at the speed of 45 RPM on the record player. The single had one song on the A - side, which was the main song and the B-side was the secondary song or in many cases a space filler. Neil Young used 'Sugar Mountain' at least twice as a B side on his early singles. The single was usually taken from the bands current LP and promoted as a hit. The B - side could be more obscure and was not always released on the LP. This made singles collectables. The Beatles released a double A side single, Marwick called it one of the "greatest bargains of all time": Penny Lane / Strawberry fields.[90] The single cover could be a plain paper sleeve carrying the record company logo or a picture sleeve with a picture of the group or another image. Buffalo Springfield released ten singles.

EP or Extended Play Record, The EP, referred to as Extended Play record in the States. It was played at the same speed as an LP: 33⅓ and normally contained four songs and could be a collection of hit singles or a selection of songs the band put out. The Buffalo Springfield made one EP. In the UK, EPs usually had a cardboard picture sleeve similar to the ones used on LPs. There was often information about the band on the back. The Beatles released "Magical Mystery Tour" as an EP in the UK and as an LP in the US. They were able to do this by adding songs that had been released as singles in the UK and not released on LPs because the Beatles saw this as short changing the fans who had already bought the song on a single having to pay for it again on the LP. The Beatles were trendsetters and there are many instances where they broke with tradition concerning records for example the length singles in the UK was doubled from two and a half minutes to five minutes with "Hey Jude". The release of Revolver was seen as a seminal event in the history of Rock Music. Not only was the recording sound amazing but all the tracks could stand alone they were so good. No track appeared to have been included just to fill space. The Beatles saw it as a continuation of what they were doing on 'Rubber Soul'. The songs had a connection to each other and the next album the phenomenal Sergeant Pepper that was reputed to be the first real concept album in popular music. The Beatles were one of the first groups where the band members released solo albums and hit singles like; Johns rock classic 'Cold Turkey,' Paul's 'Another Day, 'George's 'My Sweet Lord' and Ringo's 'It Don't Come Easy.' Neil Young emulated this by releasing his first album while still in the Buffalo Springfield and continuing his solo projects while in CSN&Y.

LP, or Album, this was originally called an album in the UK and an LP in the States. Nowadays both terms have become common on both sides of the Atlantic. This is what people usually refer to when they say a group has a new record out. The Buffalo Springfield released three LPs while they were together. The three LPs are part of my primary sources when looking into this period of Neil Young's career. I have not researched the compilation LPs because these are usually compiled and released by the record companies after the band has split up as in the case of "Retrospective" which went platinum after the Buffalo Springfield had disbanded.. The playing times varies from 30 minutes to 45 minutes. As the progressive Rock and concept albums started to evolve groups released double albums and compilations. Whereas before an LP was a compilation of hits and fillers now one song could cover the whole side 'Sad Eyed Lady of the Lowlands' released by Dylan in 1966 being a case in point. The album became a collection of songs that the band put into a sequence, depending on what they wanted to communicate. Marwick describes Sgt Pepper as: "a dramatic cycle rather than simply a chain of songs"[91] It is important to discuss these points as vinyl is no longer the popular medium of music. In my opinion CDs are definitely not digital LPs. They are an entirely different concept and in the case of people purchasing downloads online you only have them in electronic form.

To further emphasize the special individual qualities of vinyl records, if you take Jimi Hendrix´s double album "Electric Ladyland," each side of the album was created to be a musical entity. It was designed to be heard in those segments and to give the listener four different musical experiences. When a double album like that is transferred to CD format you have four sides of a record in one continuous stream. Previously with a double album you could hear side one or side four depending on your mood or taste. This aspect has disappeared with digitalization. Sergeant Pepper released in 1967 introduced the concept where the tracks were related in intrinsic themes of Rock, MusicHhall and studio effects that seemed to flow into each other, accompanied by beautiful harmonies. The whole album is a musical trip and the closing line on side one can be interpreted in different ways: "I'd love to turn you on".

"Buffalo Springfield". Released 1966 in mono and stereo.
(Atco SD / 33-200) This was the first Buffalo Springfield LP and was released by Atlantic in 1966. The first edition did not have the hit single For What its Worth on. This was added later when it was reissued in 1967. "For what it is worth" replaced the track "Baby don't scold me". The reissued album cover was identical except for the new track list. In Europe these records were released by Atlantic the mother company of Atco. The front cover photos are taken by Ivan Nagy and show the five band members faces made to look like contact prints. This effect frames their faces with the perforated edges of the negative. This is similar to the effect used by the Beatles for the cover of their "Hard Days Night" album. The Beatles' pictures are in black and white. While the Buffalo Springfield album is in color. The back cover has five white boxes on a black background:

The first box across the top half show the band in a black and white photograph. In this picture Neil Young has his eyes closed and his head is resting on the shoulder of Ritchie Furay. Bruce Palmer, the another Canadian, is looking down. The third Canadian Dewey Martin and the two Americans Ritchie Furay and Stephen Stills are looking straight at the camera.

The second box has some comments about the individual band members under each picture. For Neil Young it says: "Lead guitarist, Brown and Green, Leather and Suede, midnight, Scorpio, free, deep and dark, Winnipeg, hot and cold, wild sense of humor, hearses". It was a novelty at the time to say something about the bands personal preferences. As this is a first album people did not know very much about them. Already here you can see by Neil's pose in the picture (asleep) and some of his preferences: "Deep and Dark" and "Brown and Green," "Leather and Suede" He is already starting to cultivate "the silent type" insecure little boy image that some women find attractive. "Leather and Suede" has a connection to what I am researching as leather plays a major role in the Native American image and the buckskin jackets have a similarity to suede. The reference to 'Hearses' is because Neil Young always drove one in Canada where Stills and Young first met. He drove one to LA with Bruce Palmer. There were rollers in the back and they were perfect for transporting a bands amplifier. It was how Stills and Furay recognized Young and Palmer in LA. They were driving in a Hearst with Ontario number plates: Bruce Palmer is another band member who uses the Native American look. His image was more in the form of Calico shirts and fringed leggings. In the notes about him it says: "bass guitarist, mysterious, deep, Zen, beaded moccasins, Virgo, purple, the unknown factor, wise, safe, strong, inscrutable. " Here already on the first album is a direct reference to the Native American with "beaded moccasins." The colour purple was a popular colour among the Apache. On the picture on the back Palmer appears to be wearing a Calico shirt. The one he is wearing on the second album cover is purple. I mention Bruce Palmer in some detail because he had played together with Neil in the "Mynah Birds" in Canada and they drove down to LA together so it is quite possible that they influenced each other's dress style. The last three boxes are in the bottom third of the cover. There is one on each side listing the songs. In the middle there is the title "Buffalo Springfield" with a box underneath giving production details and the name of the record company.

These notes about band members endeared them to some fans that were not familiar with them. On the Rusties Website under "Rusties Neil's beginning" where fans put their recollections of their first encounters with Neil Young's music one Rustie wrote "I was sitting in our kitchen and listening to a radio program with US Billboard charts. They played For What its Worth and I immediately liked it. So a while later I went to town looking for the Buffalo Springfield LP. I bought it and brought it home only to find out it was the second editions cover with "FWIW"(For What It's Worth) listed as the first song but inside was the first editions record without "FWIW". I was quite disappointed, but I liked the record. I found the remarks on the musicians on the back quite strange". [92]

This statement confirms that the remarks about the musicians was a novel idea and it made a lasting impression on some people and that the first and second editions of the first record were different.

"Buffalo Springfield Again" Released in 1967 on Atco. (Atco SD 33-226). The second Buffalo Springfield album where the front cover is a photo collage illustrated by Eve Babitz and designed by Loring Eutemey.

It has a white border with pink and yellow roses and other flowers entwining with leaves. The title Buffalo Springfield Again is written inside the border across the top in bold black archaic lettering. The main picture background is a painting of a fjord with mountains on one side and some trees growing on rocky terrain in the foreground. The five members of the band are superimposed on the picture so you see the top half of their bodies on top of the mountain. They have their arms crossed in front of them holding hands with each other in a line. From left to right: Ritchie Furay is dressed in a brown suit with white shirt. He is looking straight ahead and smiling. Dewey Martin is in a black suit with white shirt and tie. He is looking to one side and slightly down and smiling. Neil Young has what appears to be a buckskin shirt or jacket on. One can see a lace up front but not the tassels. It appears similar to the one he wore on the program for the Monterey Pop Festival which had short tassels on the arm.[93]

He is looking down the mountain and into the water. He is in the "golden mean"position in the picture. There is a large pink and blue Bluebird behind him and the bird's head is between his head and Stephen Still's head. The bird is holding a blue flower that is by Neil's right ear (one of the songs on the album is called "Bluebird"). Above the Bluebird by the top of the picture, there is a break in the sky showing bright light. This light casts a reflection in the water in front of Dewy Martin. Stephen Stills in dressed in a light grey suit and white shirt, he is looking down in the same direction as Neil namely into the water. Bruce Palmer has his back to the camera looking to his right. He is dressed in a bright purple Calico shirt in the style worn by Apaches. He has what appears to be a pipe in his mouth. He is holding on to a blond angel dressed in Blue and suspended in the trees at the edge of the picture. In the left corner of the picture there is a butterfly.

The theme of the cover is very much in the spirit of 1967, Summer of Love. Lots of big flowers, angels and butterflies. The beauty of nature a calm sea. The positioning of the band is symbolic : On top of the mountain, a high point in their career. Neil and Stephen looking down in appreciation of the hard climb. Ritchie Furay looking forward enjoying the ride. Dewey Martin also appreciating the ascent. Dark mysterious Bruce Palmer smoking a pipe and connected to something spiritual in the form of an angel. Various people and bands who have inspired them along with Ringo's drumming is acknowledged on the back of the sleeve of their second album. The track "Broken Arrow" on the album was written after Neil left the group in 1967 and rejoined again. It took 100 takes to make and Neil acknowledges a lot of help from the engineer Jim Messina. Ritchie Furay tries to define the difference between Stephen Stills accessible songwriting style and Neil Young's style: "what you got from Neil's songs was, "This is my life." There always was and always will be that mystique about him. You might think you know the guy but you're not sure you really know him."[94] It was on this album that Neil was becoming more confident about singing his own songs but some people still had reservations. As Bruce palmer explains: "Neil's voice is a voice and it isn't a voice. It's a mystery but must hit some cerebral point in our sub consciousness. You can't define it." Ahmet Ertegun was less complementary about the lack of commercial appeal in Neil's voice he said to Charlie Green in the recording studio: "Hey man, Neil can't sing" to which Green replied,"He has something" Ahmet presses, "What's he got? He doesn't sing good?" (Reading this one gets the image of Tony Soprano questioning one of his underlings.) Green summed up a good definition of the appeal of Neil Young's voice at that time: "Every girl would love to nurse him to their breast, that's what he's got. He needs love and he needs mothering."[95] This description describes the image Neil was cultivating at the time perfectly. In all the songs on his first album he emphasizes this persona. Losing in love or losing his mind, helpless, lost. Elvis Presley figured out very early that not smiling and cultivating a sulky image really appealed to teenage girls. Further evidence of Neil's confidence increasing at this time can be seen when Otis Redding asked to be allowed to record Neil's song "Mr. Soul". Neil replied adamantly "Tell him I'm gonna do it". The final version has Dewey Martin singing the "faked" live intro and Neil carrying on from there. This illustrates some of the problems the band was having internal and external. Neil was confident in his abilities and his tracks from their second album are considered some of his best from that period. On January 20th the Buffalo Springfield appeared on the TV show "The Hollywood Palace" Neil sang "Mr. Soul" decked out in full Native American regalia, Comanche war jacket and beads.

'Last Time Around' Released in 1968 on Atco SD 33-256.

The third and last Buffalo Springfield album released in 1968 is appropriately named as the band no longer existed when it was released. So it was definitely the 'Last Time Around'.

The cover photograph by Gene Trindl[96] is set in an ornately wooden carved frame reminiscent of the Old West saloon doors. The groups name Buffalo Springfield is written in orange block letters on a scroll across the top in the same style as used in Buffalo Bill Wild West show posters of the 1890's. Four of the band members are standing in echelon looking to the left with Stephen Stills furthest away. Neil Young who is the first one on the right is symbolically looking in the opposite direction dressed in his fringed jacket while the others are in contemporary clothes. Inside the gatefold is the same picture cut into fragments. The back cover was designed by Derinda Christiansen and is a collage of pictures covering the band history. The theme is very Western, in the top left corner there is a large picture of Neil in his Comanche war jacket next to him is Jim Messina holding a stick and dressed in a Navajo type hat with Indian headband. Underneath them is a large sepia brown picture of a Buffalo. There are four other photos of Neil in his buckskins in the collage and one of Bruce Palmer in his purple Calico shirt taken from the second album here his buckskin leggings are also visible. The image is burnt into a piece of cowhide.[97] This album did not achieve much commercial success it got some outstanding reviews but failed to climb higher in the billboard charts than number 42. The singles taken from the album reached 107 and the second single taken from the album peaked at 82 nationwide. In Los Angeles, the single reached number 5.

Neil Young Solo "Everybody Knows this is Nowhere" Reprise Records.

His second solo album was released in 1969. It is a relevant source because of the very clear large picture of producer David Briggs dressed as a Cowboy or Outlaw. He is wearing a Cowboy hat, Western style neckerchief, jeans and cowboy boots. He is holding in the upright position a 'Winchester rifle.' The pose is very much in the style of the Déjà vu cover. He is dressed as a cowboy but like Dallas Taylor and Neil Young, he is in jeans. In a way they appear more Outlaw because Cowboys used leg guards called "Chaps." On the opposite side there are old pictures of Neil Young in his fringed jack[98]ets performing with Buffalo Springfield and by himself. This contradicts his statement earlier that he no longer wanted to be associated with the Indian image after leaving Buffalo Springfield. Here you have his producer as a rifleman and Neil portrayed as an Indian. There is one song on this LP that has a Western theme "Cowgirl in the Sand" it is a love song and none of the lyrics used have any connection to the frontier days.

THE NEIL YOUNG SONG BOOKS AS PRIMARY SOURCES.

Many aspiring folkies bought Neil young and Bob Dylan song books. They had proved that a person with a guitar could make it and if not at least they could learn enough songs to survive busking on the streets of Paris and London. The songs would be written on one page and then transcribed with the music on the next page. Above this would be a diagram showing where to put your fingers to make a chord. In this way people who could not read music could also learn the songs because they could learn the chords and then see the changes on the sheet music.

Music books are usually associated with piano and classical music. Sheet music for popular songs has been available at least from the beginning of the century. With the advent popularity of the Blues and Folk music during the early sixties it was possible to buy books with compilations of songs showing the guitar chords. As Bands became more prominent in the sixties they released books with their songs and music so aspiring guitar players could learn to play them. Normally these "song books" only contain the songs. There is no information about the band, no introduction or comments, just a discography and list of contents. These books would not be as common among fans as books about Neil Young because they are music instruction books. They can be very good for researchers looking for visual source material. The books are usually in an A4 format lavishly illustrated with large black and white or colour photos.

Each song says the title at the top and the composer. This was important because sometimes bands covered the songs of other artists. At the bottom would be the date and copywrite. There are two main volumes of Neil Young songs from this period that are worth examing.

Neil Young the Complete Music Volume 1 (1966 – 1969)
Published by Warner bros. 1974 priced at $19.95.

This book is only printed in black and white. It has five pictures on the cover: two of the Buffalo Springfield and three close ups of Neil Young smiling. This is a bit strange as Neil Young cultivated the image of the loner, a sulky distant person, hurt in love, little boy lost. He has cultivated this image in publicity photographs and on album covers for example "After the Gold Rush" where he looks sad walking on the cover. Inside the gatefold sleeve he is laying on a couch looking bored and unfulfilled surrounded by guitars. The girl in the background is lighting a cigarette. Neil Young expresses extreme sadness in some of his songs. For example in this song called Running Dry: "Oh please help me, Oh please help me, I'm livin' by myself. I need someone to comfort me, I need someone to tell. I am sorry for the things I've done, I've shamed myself with lies, But soon these things are overcome and can't be recognized.I left me love with ribbons on and water in her eyes, I took from her the love I'd won and turned it to the sky. I am sorry for the things I've done, I've shamed myself with lies, My cruelty has punctured me and now I'm running dry".

This song is the closing track on Neil Young's second solo album: 'Everybody Knows this is Nowhere'. I have quoted it in full as this song shows how the song would be written in the book and it is a perfect example of the sadness Neil Young evokes in his early work. It is played very slowly to a fiddle accompaniment reminiscent of a gypsy lament. The song is about someone who has deserted his love. He is now left full of remorse and his cruel actions have come back to haunt him. Note the line "I took from her the love I'd won and turned it to the sky". This is pure Neil Young and the action described has connotations of the Native American. It also shows how he gives associations with the nature in his songs. "I turned it to the sky", I offered it to the Great Spirit, I exposed it to the elements and set it free.

The line "I left my love with ribbons on and water in her eyes". Evokes an image of beauty, someone in ribbons, has associations with the Old West when young women always wore ribbons in their hair if they were going out. Her eyes are full with water she is overflowing and Neil is "Running Dry." It is a sad story in the style of a country song.

The first songbook comprises of 52 pictures: six double page, 30 full page, six half page photographs and ten pictures on the cover.

The back cover shows Neil Young with a big smile. One at Ritchie Furay's wedding he is wearing a Confederate Calvary uniform.[99] Next to that photo is a picture of him in his long tasseled Comanche War Jacket. The last two show the cover of "Everybody Knows this is Nowhere" and a picture of Neil alone on his bed playing the guitar.

There are nine pictures in the book of Neil Young in Native American regalia clearly showing the tasseled jacket, choker and necklace. There are three pictures of him in confederate uniform with the Buffalo Springfield and one picture of him in a Union uniform together with Jim Messina in the same uniform showing corporal strips. There is also a picture of Neil holding a Buffalo doll with an expression on his face like it is a dead animal. This could reflect on his feelings about Buffalo Springfield at the time. The book contains the songs: Broken Arrow, Cowgirl in the Sand and Last Trip to Tulsa that have references to the 'Old West' and Native Americans.

This book is very valuable as a primary source of visual references that show Neil Young in Native American regalia. There are fourteen full size clear pictures of Neil Young that can be connected to the Old West. Most of the pictures have been released in magazine articles and in books and record covers but here you have them collected in one book. Songbooks were for specialist and usually only sold in music stores that sell sheet music and books. They did not have a large circulation and twenty dollars in 1974, was a considerable amount of money for a book. As these books were not generally reprinted many of them are now out of print. With the advent of the internet where songs and sheet music can be found on free websites the demand has almost disappeared. They can be found occasionally on auction sites.

Neil Young the Complete Music Volume 2 (1969 – 1973)
Published by Warner bros. 1975 priced at $11.75.
(Price tag stuck on the back page. On Volume 1, it was printed inside)
The price here could reflect the lacking popularity of song books by 1975. I have mentioned the price was on a sticker to indicate it was not a recommended price from the publisher as in the first book. There are 47 pictures 26 single full page and 20 double page photographs plus one on the cover. There are no pictures of Neil Young in Native American regalia and

just one from the Déjà vu photo shoot that connects him to the Old West. There are two pictures of David Crosby in tasseled jacket together with CSN&Y. This could reflect on the Rolling Stone interview where Neil Young stated he had dropped the Hollywood Indian image.

The cover design is very different from the first one; it is white giving a lighter look compared to the black background of the first one. There is only one post card size picture of Neil Young alone on the cover possibly symbolizing where he was in his career. Many of the photographs inside are in elaborate color. There are seven pictures together with Crosby Stills Nash and Young. There are two pictures with his band Crazy Horse. The picture of Neil and Stray Gators used on the back of the cover of his bestselling album "Harvest" is also there. The cover from "After the Gold Rush" is included. There is a picture from the Déjà vu photo session that I describe in connection with the Déjà vu album cover shot by Tom O'Neal. This book covers a period of four years during when Neil Young released or was involved with four top selling albums. Déjà vu with CSN&Y (1969), After the Gold Rush (1970), Four Way Street with CSN&Y (1971) and Harvest solo (but with stray gators, not listed) 1972. This clearly reflects his output as an artist and is considered one of his peak periods in the Country Rock and Country Style. During the following decades he experimented with different styles, like Rock and Roll, grunge and a form of techno / Punk. He returned to this early seventies style again in the nineties. The style Neil Young used in the late sixties / early seventies, is the one that most of the sixties generation associate Neil Young with.

BILLBOARD 100, 1960 – 1968

I have taken a selection of the billboard charts to try and illustrate some of my points about the development of music in the United States. How the music changed and what was revolutionary in the sixties was that the monopoly Hollywood and the music industry had was broken in the US and the UK. People like the director of Atlantic Records Ahmet Ertegün and record companies like Tamla Motown changed the type of music played on the commercial airwaves and gave people a more widespread selection of music. The British Invasion of the American charts resulted in the development of more American groups forming. If you look at the Billboard charts one prominent feature about the charts in 1960 is there are only 20 bands out of 100 songs the rest are performed by solo artists. I have taken some examples from the Billboard 100 Charts 1960 – 1968, that have some relevance to my thesis. They are either songs with a Native American theme or they are artists that had some influence on the time. Roy Orbison for example was admired by Neil Young. All the British bands make it clear to see how the British Invasion influenced and contributed to the change that happened during that period.

1960

04. Running Bear » Johnny Preston

15. El Paso » Marty Robbins

20. Only The Lonely » Roy Orbison

42. Mr. Custer » Larry Verne

44. Mule Skinner Blues » Fendermen

96. Mule Bitty Girl » Bobby Rydell

1961

35. Apache » Jorgen Lngmann

1962

63. The Man Who Shot Liberty Valance » Gene Pitney

100. Surfin' Safari » Beach Boys

The Beach boys are mentioned in the Neil Young song "Long may you Run" entered the charts in 1962 with 'Surfin Safari'.

The theme song from the popular Western starring John Wayne: 'The Man Who Shot Liberty Valance' is evidence that Westerns were still popular at that time.

1963

By 1963 the number of bands in the US Billboard Charts have almost doubled in three years to 39 bands.

02. Surfin' U.S.A. » Beach Boys

16. Puff (The Magic Dragon) » Peter, Paul & Mary

17. Blowin' In The Wind » Peter, Paul & Mary

36. Surfer Girl » Beach Boys

37. If I Had A Hammer » Trini Lopez

45. Mean Woman Blues » Roy Orbison

59. In Dreams » Roy Orbison

69. (You're The) Devil In Disguise » Elvis Presley

80. Ring Of Fire » Johnny Cash

95. Bossa Nova Baby » Elvis Presley

97. Shut Down » Beach Boys

The British Invasion 1964

The British invasion has started with the Beatles in the vanguard spearheading the attack with 10 records in the charts plus two of their compositions recorded by other UK artists. There are 26 British singles in the billboard 100. They are predominantly Merseyside groups like Gerry and the Pacemakers and Billy J. Kramer.

1964

01. Want To Hold Your Hand » Beatles

02. She Loves You » Beatles

04. Oh, Pretty Woman » Roy Orbison

05. I Get Around » Beach Boys

13. A Hard Day's Night » Beatles

14. Love Me Do » Beatles

15. Do Wah Diddy Diddy » Manfred Mann

16. Please Please Me » Beatles

18. Little Children » Billy J. Kramer & The Dakotas

23. Glad All Over » Dave Clark Five

30. A World Without Love » Peter & Gordon

35. Wishin' And Hopin' » Dusty Springfield

38. The House Of The Rising Sun » Animals

40. Twist And Shout » Beatles

45. Bits And Pieces » Dave Clark Five

49. Don't Let The Sun Catch You Crying » Gerry & The Pacemakers

52. Can't Buy Me Love » Beatles

55. Do You Want To Know A Secret » Beatles

59. Diane » Bachelors

63. Because » Dave Clark Five

67. Can't You See That She's Mine » Dave Clark Five

73. It's Over » Roy Orbison

78. You Really Got Me » Kinks

87. Don't Throw Your Love Away » Searchers

89. How Do You Do It! » Gerry & The Pacemakers

91. Do You Love Me » Dave Clark Five

95. I Saw Her Standing There » Beatles

97. Bad To Me » Billy J. Kramer & The Dakotas

100. Needles And Pins » Searchers

1965

In 1965 The Rolling Stones who Buffalo Springfield would later support at the Hollywood Bowl are in the American charts with two hits. They are supported by a strong presence of 30 hits from UK bands. Beatles have three hits and Bob Dylan has gone electric with 'Like a Rolling Stone.' The Byrd's present an electric version of Dylan's Mr. Tambourine man along with the Loving Spoonful and the Turtles you can see a reaction to the 'British Invasion' has started.

03. (I Can't Get No) Satisfaction » Rolling Stones

06. Downtown » Petula Clark

07. Help! » Beatles

08. Can't You Hear My Heartbeat » Herman's Hermits

09. Crying In The Chapel » Elvis Presley

11. Help Me, Rhonda » Beach Boys

16. I Got You Babe » Sonny & Cher

19. Mrs. Brown You've Got A Lovely Daughter » Herman's Hermits

22. Silhouettes » Herman's Hermits

23. I'll Never Find Another You » Seekers

25. Mr. Tambourine Man » Byrds

28. What's New Pussycat? » Tom Jones
29. Eve Of Destruction » Barry McGuire
31. Ticket To Ride » Beatles
34. Game Of Love » Wayne Fontana & The Mindbenders
36. I Know A Place » Petula Clark
41. Like A Rolling Stone » Bob Dylan
42. I'm Telling You Now » Freddie & The Dreamers
43. Ferry Cross The Mersey » Gerry & The Pacemakers
46. I'm Henry VIII, I Am » Herman's Hermits
48. For Your Love » Yardbirds
49. California Girls » Beach Boys
50. Go Now » Moody Blues
51. Goldfinger » Shirley Bassey
54. Catch Us If You Can » Dave Clark Five
55. Eight Days A Week » Beatles
60. Tired Of Waiting For You » Kinks
62. All Day And All Of The Night » Kinks
64. It's Not Unusual » Tom Jones
67. Wonderful World » Herman's Hermits
69. Heart Full Of Soul » Yardbirds
70. Love Potion Number Nine » Searchers
72. Baby Don't Go » Sonny & Cher
73. It Ain't Me Babe » Turtles
74. Tell Her No » Zombies
75. I Go To Pieces » Peter & Gordon
80. I Like It Like That » Dave Clark Five
82. True Love Ways » Peter & Gordon
86. We Gotta Get Out Of This Place » Animals
88. The Last TIme » Rolling Stones
89. Do You Believe In Magic » Lovin' Spoonful

1966

In 1966 'The Ballad of the Green Berets' is at number one reflecting on the Vietnam War. Mamas and Papas have two hits 'Monday Monday' and 'California Dreaming', signalling that 'Flower Power' is on its way. The Beatles have four hits, 'Paul Revere and the Raiders' three hits. 'Loving Spoonful' three hits. One can see here a stronger emergence of American bands including the Monkees a synthetic band specifically created to counter the Beatles. 'The Hollies' featuring Graham Nash later of Crosby, Stills &Nash, appear with their hit 'Bus Stop'. This is the exciting and musically competitive environment that The Buffalo Springfield released their first album into.

01. The Ballad Of The Green Berets » Sgt. Barry Sadler
06. Last Train To Clarksville » Monkees

07. Monday, Monday » Mama's & The Papa's
10. California Dreamin' » Mama's & The Papa's
11. Summer In The City » Lovin' Spoonful
16. We Can Work It Out » Beatles
21. Paint It Black » Rolling Stones
22. My Love » Petula Clark
24. Wild Thing » Troggs
25. Kicks » Paul Revere & The Raiders
26. Sunshine Superman » Donovan
27. Sunny » Bobby Hebb
28. Paperback Writer » Beatles
33. Good Vibrations » Beach Boys
34. A Groovy Kind Of Love » Mindbenders
35. You Don't Have To Say You Love Me » Dusty Springfield
41. Daydream » Lovin' Spoonful
45. Bus Stop » Hollies
51. I Am A Rock » Simon & Garfunkel
54. The Sounds Of Silence » Simon & Garfunkel
55. Lady Godiva » Peter & Gordon
56. Did You Ever Have To Make Up Your Mind? » Lovin' Spoonful
57. You Baby » Turtles
59. Homeward Bound » Simon & Garfunkel
61. Bang Bang » Cher
62. Sloop John B » Beach Boys
63. 19th Nervous Breakdown » Rolling Stones
67. Just Like Me » Paul Revere & The Raiders
79. Barbara Ann » Beach Boys
82. Rainy Day Women #12 And 35 » Bob Dylan
87. Woman » Peter & Gordon
90. Nowhere Man » Beatles
91. Dandy » Herman's Hermits
96. Yellow Submarine » Beatles
97. Hungry » Paul Revere & The Raiders
99. Shapes Of Things » Yardbirds

The summer of love 1967

You can clearly see the dominance here of the progressive rock music emerging to a dominant position in the charts. Among them the Buffalo Springfield 'For What its worth'. It is noticeable that their single is the only protest song in the charts at that time. This is significant because throughout his career Neil Young has always made protest songs about issues he felt strongly about. He has a strong sense of right and wrong that comes through in his songs most recently with 'Let's Roll' that he was inspired to write after 9/11 when he heard the story of the resistance put up by Todd Beamer and the passengers on United Airlines flight 93.

I have included everything that could be of relevance to mark the UK contribution of 1967 notably; The Beatles, 'All You Need is Love' and Procol Harum, 'Whiter Shade of Pale.'

And the emergence of 'Flower Power bands' from San Francisco and LA like 'The Jefferson Airplane' with the song 'White Rabbit' and 'The, Turtles' with 'Happy Together.'

Songs like these represent the year and the era. When they are mixed with the Soul Classics listed below, they define the feeling of 1967 'The Summer of Love' there is something musically for everyone 'Ode to Billie Joe' for the 'Country Music Lovers,' 'I'm a Believer' for the teenyboppers. 'Something Stupid', 'Green Green Grass of Home' and 'Release Me' for the 'Mature Generation.' This was one of the few occasions in the sixties when everyone was included. This aspect must have made a vast contribution to the 'Good Vibrations' that went round during the 'Summer of Love.' It is noticeable that there were four theme tunes from films in the charts that year and all of those films had social realistic themes: 'To Sir With Love' with Sidney Portiere was about a Black school teacher in a predominately white London school. The film 'Alfie,' starred Michael Cain as a male gigolo photographer working in London. The theme song was sung by Millicent Martin on the UK release and Cher on the US copy of the film. Some pretty amazing jazz was released during this period and the rest of the soundtrack of the film 'Alfie' is by jazz saxophonist Sonny Rollins. The Academy award winning film 'Georgie Girl' represented the change in the times regarding peoples relationships. It involved two women, one with a baby, a lover, and an elderly gentleman. 'The Happening' was an anti-establishment movie questioning the values of the older generation in Middle America. In this story, an important, influential, rich man is kidnapped and stunned to learn that no one is willing to pay the ransom.

1967

01. To Sir With Love » Lulu (Theme from the film 'To Sir with Love)
02. The Letter » Box Tops
03. Ode To Billie Joe » Bobby Gentry
04. Windy » Association
05. I'm A Believer » Monkees
06. Light My Fire » Doors
07. Somethin' Stupid » Nancy Sinatra & Frank Sinatra
08. Happy Together » Turtles
09. Groovin' » Young Rascals
13. Respect » Aretha Franklin
14. I Was Made To Love Her » Stevie Wonder
17. Sweet Soul Music » Arthur Conley
19. Soul Man » Sam & Dave

20. Never My Love » Association
23. Incense and Peppermints » Strawberry Alarm Clock
24. Ruby Tuesday » Rolling Stones
27. For What It's Worth » Buffalo Springfield
28. Gimme Little Sign » Brenton Wood
28. Love Is Here And Now You're Gone » Supremes
29. The Happening » Supremes (Theme from the film 'The Happening')
30. All You Need Is Love » Beatles
31. Release Me (And Let Me Love Again) » Engelbert Humperdinck
32. Your Precious Love » Marvin Gaye & Tammi Terrell
33. Somebody To Love » Jefferson Airplane
34. Get On Up » Esquires
35. Brown Eyed Girl » Van Morrison
36. Jimmy Mack » Martha & The Vandellas
37. I Got Rhythm » Happenings
38. A Whiter Shade Of Pale » Procol Harum
41. Reflections » Diana Ross & The Supremes
42. On A Carousel » Hollies
44. Alfie » Dionne Warwick, (Theme from the film 'Alfie')
45. San Francisco » Scott Mckenzie
45. Silence Is Golden » Tremeloes
46. My Cup Runneth Over » Ed Ames
47. Up, Up And Away » Fifth Dimension
49. The Rain, The Park And Other Things » Cowsills
50. There's A Kind Of Hush » Herman's Hermits
52. This Is My Song » Petula Clark
53. (Your Love Keeps Lifting Me) Higher and Higher » Jackie Wilson
54. I've Been Lonely Too Long » Young Rascals
55. Penny Lane » Beatles
56. You're My Everything » Temptations
57. Georgie Girl » Seekers, (Theme from the film 'Georgie Girl')
58. Western Union » Five Americans
59. Baby I Love You » Aretha Franklin
60. A Little Bit You, A Little Bit Me » Monkees
61. California Nights » Lesley Gore
62. Dedicated To The One I Love » Mama's & The Papa's
63. How Can I Be Sure » Young Rascals
64. Carrie Ann » Hollies
65. (We Ain't Got) Nothin' Yet » Blue Magoos
66. Friday On My Mind » Easy Beats
67. Soul Finger » Bar-Kays
68. Gimme Some Lovin' » Spencer Davis Group
69. Let It Out (Let It All Hang Out) » Hombres

70. Let's Live For Today » Grass Roots
71. Close Your Eyes » Peaches & Herb
72. Groovin' » Booker T & The MG's
73. Funky Broadway » Wilson Pickett
74. Pleasant Valley Sunday » Monkees
75. I Never Loved A Man (The Way I Love You) » Aretha Franklin
77. Cold Sweat » James Brown & The Famous Flames
78. She'd Rather Be With Me » Turtles
79. 98.6 » Keith
80. Here We Go Again » Ray Charles
81. White Rabbit » Jefferson Airplane
82. Bernadette » Four Tops
83. The Beat Goes On » Sonny & Cher
84. Snoopy Vs. The Red Baron » Royal Guardsmen
85. Society's Child » Janis Ian
86. Girl, You'll Be A Woman Soon » Neil Diamond
87. Ain't No Mountain High Enough » Marvin Gaye & Tammi Terrell
89. Here Comes My Baby » Tremeloes
90. Everlasting Love » Robert Knight
91. I Dig Rock And Roll Music » Peter, Paul & Mary
92. Little Ole Man (Uptight-everything's Alright) » Bill Cosby
93. I Had Too Much To Dream Last Night » Electric Prunes
94. Daydream Believer » Monkees
95. Baby I Need Your Lovin' » Johnny Rivers
97. Mirage » Tommy James & The Shondells
98. Green, Green Grass Of Home » Tom Jones
98. I Can See For Miles » Who
99. Don't Sleep In The Subway » Petula Clark
100. Thank The Lord For The Night Time » Neil Diamond

1968

The Billboard Top 100 in 1968 shows a lack of psychedelic rock. Buffalo Springfield did not have any chart successes with singles that year. The Beatles broke the mode of the three minute single with 'Hey Jude' and the Rolling Stones 'Jumping Jack Flash' hit fellow rockers like Pete Townsend like a bolt of lightning. British rock band 'Cream' had two hits with 'Sunshine of your Love' and 'White Room'. My favourite American group at that time 'Steppenwolf' also had two hits that brought them some prominence: 'Magic Carpet Ride' and 'Born to be Wild' the latter became part of the soundtrack of the film 'Easy Rider' released in 1969 ('The Pusher' by Steppenwolf was also in the film). If you look through the following 81 songs that I have selected out of the top 100 Billboard chart you cannot help but appreciate the amount of creativity that was going around in 1968. I think most people would agree there were some pretty amazing sounds coming over the airwaves back in 1968. Modern digital reproductions somehow cannot completely capture the atmosphere of the scuffed up singles stacked in the mono Dansette record player. (Those were the days my friend.)

01. Hey Jude » Beatles
02. Love Is Blue » Paul Mauriat
04. (Sittin' On) The Dock Of The Bay » Otis Redding
05. People Got To Be Free » Rascals
06. Sunshine Of Your Love » Cream
08. The Good, The Bad And The Ugly » Hugo Montenegro
09. Mrs. Robinson » Simon & Garfunkel
11. Harper Valley P.T.A. » Jeannie C. Riley
12. Little Green Apples » O.C. Smith
14. Hello, I Love You » Doors
15. Young Girl » Gary Puckett & the Union Gap
16. Cry Like A Baby » Box Tops
17. Stoned Soul Picnic » Fifth Dimension
18. Grazing In The Grass » Hugh Masekela
19. Midnight Confessions » Grass Roots
20. Dance To The Music » Sly & The Family Stone
22. I Wish It Would Rain » Temptations
23. La-La Means I Love You » Delfonics
25. Judy In Disguise (With Glasses) » John Fred & His Playboy Band
27. Love Child » Diana Ross & The Supremes
28. Angel Of The Morning » Merrilee Rush
29. The Ballad Of Bonnie And Clyde » Georgie Fame
30. Those Were The Days » Mary Hopkins
31. Born To Be Wild » Steppenwolf
32. Cowboys To Girls » Intruders
33. Simon Says » 1910 Fruit Gum Company
34. Lady Willpower » Gary Puckett & The Union Gap
35. A Beautiful Morning » Rascals
36. The Look Of Love » Sergio Mendes & Brasil '66
38. Yummy, Yummy, Yummy » Ohio Express
39. Fire » Crazy World Of Arthur Brown
40. Love Is All Around » Troggs
42. (Theme From) Valley Of The Dolls » Dionne Warwick
43. Classical Gas » Mason Williams
44. Slip Away » Clarence Carter
46. (Sweet Sweet Baby) Since You've Been Gone » Aretha Franklin
47. Green Tambourine » Lemon Pipers
48. 1, 2, 3, Red Light » 1910 Fruit Gum Company
50. Jumpin' Jack Flash » Rolling Stones
51. MacArthur Park » Richard Harris

52. Light My Fire » Jose Feliciano
54. Take Time To Know Her » Percy Sledge
55. Pictures Of Matchstick Men » Status Quo
56. Summertime Blues » Blue Cheer
57. Ain't Nothing Like The Real Thing » Marvin Gaye & Tammi Terrell
58. I Got The Feelin' » James Brown & The Famous Flames
59. I've Gotta Get A Message To You » Bee Gees
60. Lady Madonna » Beatles
61. Hurdy Gurdy Man » Donovan
62. Magic Carpet Ride » Steppenwolf
82. You're All I Need To Get By » Marvin Gaye & Tammi Terrell
83. Baby, Now That I've Found You » Foundations
84. Sweet Inspiration » Sweet Inspirations
85. If You Can Want » Smokey Robinson & The Miracles
88. Do You Know The Way To San Jose » Dionne Warwick
89. Scarborough Fair / Canticle » Simon & Garfunkel
90. Say It Loud I'm Black And I'm Proud » James Brown & Famous Flames
91. The Mighty Quinn » Manfred Mann
92. Here Comes The Judge » Shorty Long
93. I Say A Little Prayer » Aretha Franklin
94. Think » Aretha Franklin
95. Sealed With A Kiss » Gary Lewis & The Playboys
96. Piece Of My Heart » Big Brother & The Holding Company
97. Suzie Q. » Creedence Clearwater Revival
98. Bend Me Shape » American Breed
99. Hey, Western Union Man » Jerry Butler
100. Never Give You Up » Jerry Butler
63. Bottle Of Wine » Fireballs
66. Delilah » Tom Jones
68. I Thank You » Sam & Dave
69. The Fool On The Hill » Sergio Mendes & Brasil '66
70. Sky Pilot » Eric Burdon & The Animals
71. Indian Lake » Cowsills
73. Over You » Gary Puckett & The Union Gap
74. Goin' Out Of My Head / Can't Take My Eyes Off You » Lettermen
75. Shoo-Bee-Doo-Be-Doo-Da-Day » Stevie Wonder
77. (You Keep Me) Hangin' On » Vanilla Fudge
78. Revolution » Beatles
79. Woman, Woman » Gary Puckett & The Union Gap
80. Eleanor » Turtles
81. White Room » Cream

RUSTIES.

The Rusties is made up of a group of people who follow Neil Young's career or are fans. They have an internet site on Yahoo that anyone can apply to join. The following statements are selection from an appeal I made to them for material during my research. I asked for any reminisces or knowledge of connections between Neil young and Native Americans. I added the dimension of what his music meant to them personally to try and give a wider approach. The Rusties are a community where there is of course a focus on what Neil young is doing at the present time and any news about re-releases or people who want information about some obscure event connected to music history or Neil Young's career or up an coming tour dates. On top of that they discuss everything like films or cheap airline tickets or magazines. The virtual community spirit you find here is very reflective of the community spirit present at some Neil Young concerts. For example the striking thing I noticed while at a Neil Young concert in Berlin was the kind of 'vibe' that the people attending the concert gave off. It is quite hard to put into words, they kind of looked like they had all taken different routes through life and still ended up with the standard conventional goals, like jobs, kids and cars and somehow along the way they had managed to retain a youthfulness in their demure. There was a definite 'something' in that demure that seemed to bind them into a kind of fellowship. Of course part of it could be most of the people who go to his concerts know the music inside out. I cannot really formulate the 'vibe' into words but it was definitely there. Whatever song Neil Young pulls out of the hat at a concert with "here is an old song", the Rusties are right on it and you can read on the site which album that song is on or where it comes from. Because of some of these references I have left the correspondence that I got from the Rusties more of less intact. I have trimmed off anything too irrelevant and left anything I felt contributed to what this book is about or reflected on that era. I am most grateful to the Rusties who took the time to write to me. Although they are written in the present I hope you will view these letters (written by primary sources who were actually there) as historical documentation of the events that spread over half a century.

Tim, wrote, Feb. 4th, 2009: "Neil has said that he believes there is a connection between Native Americans and Nature. He wants to keep that spirit going. If you've ever been to Farm Aid or the Bridge School Benefit shows, then you've seen either Chief Dennis, his daughter Denise or his grandson (name escapes me) open those concerts with ritual Indian dancing. Chief Dennis has passed on now, but his spirit continues through his child, and her child. Rustie Kathy Popple hippie girl smile knows more than most about that subject. Neil still has the American Indian presence on stage with him and his family and friends when he tours. That would be his wooden cigar store Indian that seems to always be there, with his heart glowing. That is all over rust in pictures. Chrome Dreams II had a number of songs relating to spirituality, especially walking in the tall trees...that's Neil chapel...the red woods...nature". Tim mentions some other interesting connections between Neil young and the Native Americans. Between the Farm aid and Bridge School benefits and Chief Denis. He gives the name of a Rusty who 'knows more than most.' Tim mentions a cigar store Indian that can be seen in 'Rust' (Rust Never Sleeps 1979). Neil Young has used the Indian since the early seventies.[100] Chrome Dreams II is from 2007 Neil says, "Some early listeners have said that this album is positive and spiritual. I like to think it focuses on the human condition"[101] so Tim's information coincides with what Neil Young has said. "Neil's chapel: the Red Woods, nature." This is a good interpretation of what Neil is trying to communicate to his audience. People who like him appear to sincerely believe in his intentions and some of his philosophy about life.

Louis, wrote, April 6, 2009: "Wisdom Dancers opened the last 5, 10, Farm Aids, I really don't know how many... Chief Dennis Alley became "blood brothers" with Willie Nelson in a ceremony then a year or two later became "blood brothers" with Neil before a Farm Aid (one rustie witnessed this, but I don't want to out her... if you want me to ask her if she will comment on it off rust, I will)... I met Dennis twice, very nice guy... he died a year or two ago, unfortunately... He was the leader of the Wisdom Dancers and many of its members (maybe all) are from his family... I did buy a t-shirt that was my favourite ever, it was the native American on the Indian at the "End of the Trail" with the full moon in the background... a rustie had me mail it to him and he took a picture of it and used it for cover art on one of the shows, but I don't remember the rustie, but should still have the cover art somewhere... I gave the shirt away in Kenya, Africa, and now regret it... I do have one very cool poster that I doubt you have seen, let me see if I can attach it... ok, found two different versions, one a bit darker than the other... and one has the back (also attached) which is a map to the concert... a very early Crazy Horse show, maybe March of 1970, at Contra Costa College (you could find it on Tom Hamilton's Sugar Mountain site)" Louis contributes with some interesting points: He confirms Tim's information and comes with some names: Wisdom Dancers open for Neil Young sometimes. Chief Dennis Alley made Neil a 'Blood Brother' these points are confirmed by other Rusties. Louise mentions the Neil Young 'End of the Trail' T-shirt which is probably based on a Remington sculpture which is now considered a very rare classic. He gives details of a poster from 1970, with Crazy Horse naming college and possible date along with a website that may have further information. I communicated a few times with Louis and like most of the Rusties I had contacted he was always helpful, coming with suggestions. The Rusties seem to have adopted some of the sixties values of sharing and looking out for each other. Note how Louis says a Rustie witnessed the event but he does not want to 'out 'her, meaning reveal her name without her permission. He sent me some scans of the poster and I sent him a scan of a Neil Young T-shirt that he identified as 'The Moving Rider on the Horse.' Note how he gave away his favourite Neil Young T-shirt away in Africa. Although he regrets it now it did not end up in the cupboard, it took on a new life, this was part of the 'Diggers' idea with 'Free Shops,' you give away what you don't use and other people that can use it, take it, and donate what they are not using. That way we consume less and we would preserve more of our natural resources. Louis's 'End of the Trail' T-shirt might have ended up adorning a Messiah Warrior on the slopes of Kilimanjaro!

Carol, wrote, April 5th 2009: "I feel that there are many Americans that have deepest respect for the True Americans. There are always the few who don't care. I for one love the people that I have met. They do honour the flag, yes. Here is the scoop on the opening ceremony. The Native Americans open with a dance, and a blessing made now by Denise Alley, since her father died. Being that this show, Farm Aid and Bridge have so many acts, that the crowd is sparse for the opening, which is too bad."

"The closing however is just the opposite. Willy Nelson closes the actual show, Then Denise and the group come out and do the closing finale. Very great!! almost everyone is still in their seats. Did you know that Chief Denis and Neil are blood brothers? and Dave Matthews is Denis' adopted son? It was done in a ritual when Denis was well. I saw a picture of the gravestone....... It says blood brother Neil Young, and adopted son Dave Matthews. Then the rest of immediate survivors".

Carol's message confirms what Louis said about the 'Blood Brother' and that Denise Alley now opens the show for the Wisdom Dancers (also mentioned by Louis). Carol gives information of a primary source in the form of a gravestone that gives details of a connection between Neil Young and the Native Americans. This is obviously a personal matter and not anything that Neil Young has done to promote his work as an artist. Carol wrote a second message when I asked her to give some more details. Here Carol amplifies on her first letter about what a great experience it was and how she got to know some of the dancers. Louis also got to meet Chief Denis personally and Carol describes them as wonderful people. Carol give the exact year that Chief Denis passed away in (2007). Carol's friend Kathy knows the Denis family well and through her Carol was invited into the inner circle and learned more about the Wisdom Dancers.

Carol's second message, 5th April: "I was lucky enough to have seen the Native Americans dance at the opening, and at the closing of Farm Aid, and Bridge school Benefit last fall. I got to spend some time with them also. I must say that it was very beautiful to hear and watch. I also got to share a room at Farm Aid with Denise Alley, daughter of chief Denis Alley who passed away in 2007. There were quite a few in the dance group, and they stayed at the same hotel where I stayed. It was a wonderful experience to have shared this time with them. My friend Kathy HGS is a great friend of Denise Alley, and Chief Denis. That is how I got to meet them. They are wonderful people. Denise and the dancers open the show, and at the end they do the closing dance. This is done at Farm Aid and Bridge School. I am so happy to have met and shared time with them".

Marilyn wrote, April 5th, 2009: The points about Farm Aid are very relevant because they show how the Native American element is still very much connected to Neil Young when he is on his home turf doing Farm Aid and Bridge School Benefits. This message from Marilyn gives more confirmation about Chief Dennis and the farm aid. Marilyn mentions a website and another Rustie, 'Kathy Hippie Girl Smile'. Who is the friend mentioned in Carol's letter. This shows how the Rusties are connected to each other. A good source was Neil Young's film Human Highway that contains the scene she mentions where Neil Dances with Native Americans round a fire. "you may look at the farm aid website, BSB, (Bridge School Benefit) website and YouTube for videos of Dennis and his family at both farm aid and BSB...Kathy hippie girl on this list was friends with Dennis, who passed away last year, I believe. Dennis and his family are Native dancers...This is my favourite 'Native American and Neil' that I have had the privilege of seeing....it is from Neil's movie, Human Highway, and is part of the 'dream sequence' I love how happy Neil looks to be dancing around the fire with those folks, sharing song..."

Dionys, wrote, April5 2009: "A couple of years ago I did an interview with the late Floyd Westerman about his appearance in the Dances With Wolves movie. The two buffalo which were used to do the hunting stunt scenes in that movie were owned by Neil Young. One of them was named "Cody" (after Buffalo Bill), the other was named "mammoth". One of these animals liked salted crackers very much. So when you approached the animal and shook a cracker box, the buffalo got down and "wallowed" on the ground. That's why it could be used for these scenes. So Neil supported the making of this movie. Neil also appeared at the Paha Sapa II concert in the 90's, although I do not know very much about this concert." I got this message from a journalist living in Germany called Dionys. He mentions the name of Neil's Buffalo "Cody" and connects it to 'Buffalo Bill'. He states that Neil supported Dancing with Wolves, this film is one of my primary sources. The mention of Paha Sapa II is a benefit concert played on the Pine Ridge reservation radio station "KILI".[102] As I have previously mentioned Buffalo are a big factor in Neil Young's career and it is fitting that he should contribute to the preservation of the 'Thunder Beast'. The mention of the late Floyd Westerman show how important it is to record these recollections and memories while people are still around. A full interview of something like this would be an excellent source.

Jon, wrote, April 5ᵗʰ, 2009: I got this message from Jon where he says he thinks he might have seen the Buffalo Springfield in the late 1960's, supporting Lee Michaels. I have a friend in the UK who saw Jimi Hendrix in a youth club in London before he became popular. There was only about 50 kids in the audience aged about 14. The clubs Jon mentions in CA are a good source of information and the possibility of Neil using Indian acts on a solo tour. Even though he is not certain he confirms what the other 'Rusties' have said about the Bridge Concerts.

"Although I became a fan of BS, (Buffalo Springfield) back in the late 60's, I never saw them live. I did go to some of the venues they played and may have even met them. I also may have seen them at The Ark in Sausalito, CA. They opened for Lee Michaels and I saw him a lot. This was before I got into BS. I do remember a group with fringe jackets and thought they sounded pretty good. I would have been there for Lee though, I do remember a concert a few years ago in Berkeley. It was a Neil solo tour. I believe he had a couple of Indian acts for him. I definitely have seen the Indians open at Bridge. Again, I'm not a big fan of Indian music so it was sort of a throwaway to me at a show. I do believe in what the Indians represent. Respect for what "God" has given us." As Jon had been around in the late 1960's I wrote to him and asked if he could amplify how things were in the US back then to help me get a better picture

Jon, wrote April 6, 2009: "I remember growing up and seeing Indians in my hometown. They were usually a very proud people, but highly susceptible to the drink. My father wouldn't serve them alcohol and he was never a prejudiced man. I feel that Indians got more respect during the 60's, along with Blacks, Mexicans, Filipinos and other cultures. Mainly it was simply the "We are all one" thinking that went in the period. There is plenty of info on that. Nowadays I rarely see anyone I can easily say is an Indian. That would include the casinos. In case you don't know, the US Government granted the Indians the right to open casinos on their land. This increased the wealth to those in charge of the tribes but didn't trickle down well. Sort of like any government." Jon's second letter reflects the sentiment of growing up in America at that time. It is an interesting point in the description of the father not serving alcohol. This appears very bigoted today but in history you cannot use today's modern values for judgement. When people do something out of the ordinary or in a different way they are contributing to a change of attitude. What Jon's father did at that time could also be interpreted as a compassionate act. Jon tells how he experienced the Native Americans along with other ethnic minorities getting more respect during the sixties. The 'We are all one' feeling of unity there was during that period. I have left in the part about the Casinos because it is very topical in the media at the moment and mention it later in a discussion. Jon makes a good point 'sort of like any government'. Sometimes people expect Indians to be different because they are a tribe and are disappointed when they act just like everyone else. Obviously these days any form of self-government has to incorporate a compulsory tax system to serve the community. In an open democratic system like Scandinavia where they usually have higher taxes they give bigger subsides back to the community in the form of education and health care. During the Thatcher era in the UK where she made the rich richer and proved the trickledown effect does not work. So there is nothing new in that situation.

Thomas, wrote, April 6ᵗʰ, 2009: "You asked about the hippies at the Haight-Ashbury district and how it may have related to Native Americans. My limited experience was when I was 18 and was in the army at Fort Ord in 1968. Spent about 10 weekends in the district with a friend I met who was from Frisco. The contrast between a kid from Indianapolis and the hippy's was overwhelming. I can see a correlation between what the flower children were trying to do and the NA. They would sit in front of the store front windows they had taken over at night and sit in a circle. They would pass their version of the peace pipe around the circle and listen to their music and dance like the NA used to do in their tents and fires. I guess you could say they were trying to get that lifestyle back.

As for my memories of Neil back then I discovered him in 1968 listening to the BS knowing who anyone in the band was at the time. When found out who was singing in that weird voice that had hooked me his records, concerts and any words written about him became an event in my life. The first time I heard Helpless I knew I had found the real deal I could not believe someone that young could produce something so beautiful. The first concert was around 1972-73, at the Convention Centre in Indianapolis it was my first real rock concert and the thought of seeing Neil for the first time was exciting. I went with my wife and another couple who were veterans of concerts. My wife was a country girl just turning 20 a few weeks before the concert when the lights went down and the matches and lighters came out and people were lighting up my wife saw two policemen a few feet away and said those people are going to get arrested then noticed the three of us were partaking. When Neil came out and was sitting on a stool looking like a mountain man the way he was dressed my eyes were fixed on him after hearing most of Harvest and the unreleased songs from Time Fades A way. I looked forward to the next time he came to town which was not until the Solo Trans tour and by that time Neil and I had gone through several different changes. Hope this helps you if you need some more rock and NA music listen to Robbie Robertson who made two NA records and is at least part NA". Thomas's letter is a 'snapshot' of the period giving a perfect impression of what was going on at the time. This letter confirms many of the points I have been making: he was 18 in the military and hung out with the counter culture. Showing the feeling of unity there was between young people at that time and how they were able to merge with different groups. He talks about the overwhelming difference between a kid from Indianapolis (who is serving in the army) and a hippy. Those kind of situations arose back then because people were exposed to different values and attitudes. Many things contributed to these changes in the individual, music, concerts, magazines like 'Rolling Stone' in the US and 'IT' in the UK. Musicians and journalists at the time where questioning the validity of what was happening in the society. Thomas gives a good description of the hippies following NA (Native Americans) traditions. He heard BS in 1968 and was attracted to Neil Young's unusual voice. "Concerts and written words about him became part of my life from then on." He mentions Helpless that was released in 1970 when Neil is 25 and Thomas is 20 for many people like him Neil Young has been the voice of their generation. Besides reading 'written words about him' he was listening to his music and going to his concerts. Thomas is not alone; many Neil Young fans have similar backgrounds or became initiated to Neil Young the same way that he did. Neil Young expresses in his songs the troubles and the emotional turbulence young people go through and they can identify with it. As the director Jonathan Demme says; "It's just astonishing – this stuff comes from a particularly unique place in his soul and in his life, and the lyrics come from an extra – special personal dimension"[103] At 22, Thomas is with his wife and friends smoking a joint at a CSN&Y concert. Smoking joints at concerts in those days is comparable to having a beer in the intermission today, almost everyone did it. There is a good description of Neil 'looking like a mountain man' meaning standard Neil Young dress code: lumberjack shirt, jeans and boots. The year is 1972 -73, and the sixties are ending.[104] Thomas mentions Neil and himself have gone through several different changes by the 'Trans' period which was ten years later (1982). However, Thomas is a Rustie, and that is proof he is still attached to the herd, keeping one eye on what Neil is doing and releasing. He quite possibly has the archive box. Thomas is a logical candidate for the 'Archive Box' as it covers the years up to 'Trans' which is when a he says "Neil and I had gone through several different changes". Collections like the Archive Box are interesting for avid fans because it includes material that was created back then but left out. In that way it is more representative of the times than old material re-recorded today. As a final tip Thomas mentions Robbie Robinson from the Band who played with Bob Dylan. As a lead for more sources he mentions Robinson has made two NA records and has NA roots. Thomas's recollections give us a clear view from the other side. The box set 'Archives' give us a view from Neil's side of the fence. They were both going through changes and one of Neil's gifts is he is able to interpret some of these changes and put them into music so young people like Thomas growing up and going through all the trials and tribulations that involves is able to relate to them.

Lynne, wrote, May 7th, 2009: "My current husband and I have attended many, many NY shows throughout Neil's career (We nearly met one another for decades at NY concerts). My first NY solo show was the 01-27-1971, Macky Auditorium, University Of Colorado, Boulder, Colorado, show (that's my ticket stub on the Sugar Mountain site). I also attended the 05-12-1970, Denver Coliseum, Denver, Colorado, USA show w/ Crosby, Stills, Nash and Young. I had that stub but spaced it out somewhere." This gives dates of two concerts and a reference to a site 'sugarmountain.org' that lists all Neil Young's concerts. Lynne has sent in a scan of her old ticket stub from 1971, to the site and it now serves as a historical document, giving details of price $4.75 and time in the evening 8:00. The stub is torn over so you cannot read the whole date only '27, 1971' and the end of the word Auditorium (itorium). If Lynne had not sent it in with details it would be very hard to identify as it does not say Neil Young on the stub.

Lynne's second letter, May 7th, 2009: "I first heard Neil when he was with the Buffalo Springfield on their albums, listening with high school intensity in Casper, Wyoming, in 1968 and 1969. It turned out that Casper had an inside pipeline to Neil because a local couple, Shannon Forbes and David Briggs, had moved to California to sample the counter-culture, and their friends always knew the latest goings-on of the Canyon set. Shannon's family was incredibly supportive of her back in the day, so what might have felt distant was just a coffee klatch away if you knew the Forbes clan or their kin. I followed Neil through gossip and album, bringing his music to literature classes at the University of Wyoming, missing his concert with CSNY on 1969-11-26, at the Coliseum, in Denver, Colorado. Then finally connecting with CSNY in 1970-05-12, at the Denver Coliseum in Colorado, after a gruelling tale of bars and crooked police, security guards and harrowing bus rides. It was then that I realized I had become an addict. I needed a fix, so I scored two tickets for January 27th, 1971, from Dean's Music Box in Laramie, Wyoming, for $4.75 each to the Boulder show. I was 20, but you only had to be 18 to drink beer in Colorado, and it didn't matter that I didn't have a car because I hadn't learned to drive anyhow and I didn't want to hitchhike the 100 miles or so from college to civilization, so I figured I could get a ride if I had double tickets and was on a mission. I had just gotten my second semester sophomore student assist job in the Engineering College, so I was feeling rich. I asked a Neil-admiring not-boyfriend to go and I gave him my extra ticket. I helped pay for gas also, which was about 25 cents a gallon, I think. We took his new yellow Javelin down Highway 287. I had borrowed a fringed brown leather jacket that matched the brown leather fringed silver Conchos down my bell-bottom jeans and we headed to the Hill in Boulder, the center of all that was happening in a mini-Haight way. I bought a new pair of earrings and some incense at an India-Indian place on the Hill and we headed over to Macky to get in line. There were a lot of people outside, but I had never been to the venue so I didn't know what to expect. We maneuvered our way to the front of the line, and were in prime position when the doors opened at 7:00. We got seats about 6 rows back on the center left-hand stage side. The concert was sublime: Tattered jeans, scruffy mocs, faded flannel, hair covering his glorious eyes before the wickedest grins, harmonica, guitar, piano, total Neil-loving drool-slobbering monkey-gibbering bliss. I got to hear Cowgirl In the Sand, and I was in Heaven because it was MY SONG, being from Wyoming and thinking I was a cowgirl and all. I vibrated in my chair and got hoarse by not screaming, just whimpering and squealing and trying to make sure I never forgot my first real Neil Solo concert. I didn't fathom until later that the extra people milling around outside had thrown things through the windows of the venerable hall because the concert was sold out and they wanted in. I was mystified that night by Neil's reference to "this concert is by Neil Young and the Gate-crashes" or some such, and I thought it was standard procedure to exit the hall by the front of the stage. I wasn't disabused of this notion until days later when I found out about the shenanigans of the ticket less. We drove off into the moonset after the show. We were all so new to the process in 1971, that even waiting for Neil after the concert would have seemed rude, and asking how Shannon was doing would have seemed downright pushy. However, we vowed to never forget that night, and I guess I haven't yet, as it seems like yesterday to me even now." Lynne's husbands story "My husband went the night before me on January 26th, 1971. He hitchhiked up to Boulder from Denver where he was going to school at the University of Denver as a freshman. It was about 45 miles back then on the night he went. He admits he doesn't remember much except that the concert was great. It was the first time he had seen Neil. He also does not remember any civil disturbance, nor, indeed, what he did after he knocked on his future brother-in-law's apartment door looking for a place to sleep after the concert and was politely refused entry." Addendum : I have more Neil stories and Shannon Forbes stories, and more civil unrest stories of Wyoming after Kent State if you need filler, which I doubt. Thanks for your patience, and I get to see Neil with Mike at Denver University (!) on Tuesday. Ain't life strange?" Lynne's second letter gives another rich and informative 'snapshot' of the period, she has excellent recollection of the time and the trip she made. Recalling first hearing Buffalo Springfield while at high school in Casper. She gives an illuminating female view of a Neil Young concert and describes Neil as an attractive man. This is an aspect of Neil Young not often bought up by rock journalists who tend to be men. "Neil Young looked really dishy tonight as he gave a rendition of 'Sugar Mountain'...etc. A male would probably not describe Neil's eyes as glorious. Lynne obviously sees him as an attractive male 'Neil-loving drool-slobbering monkey-gibbering bliss'. I have not approached this aspect of Neil Young's image. However on the cover of Déjà vu he could be classified as tall dark and handsome in a traditional sense, the

River boat gambler Western attire adding to this image. She mentions knowing David Briggs who was Neil's producer photographed with the Winchester inside the gatefold sleeve on Everybody Knows this is Nowhere. If one knew the Forbes family one could get inside information about 'the latest goings on of the Canyon set.' By this she probably means Topanga Canyon[105] where Neil Young and David Briggs lived or Laurel Canyon where many of the music scene people lived at that time. Lynne's description of her clothes fits into the points I have made she wore: "fringed brown leather jacket that matched the brown leather fringed silver Conchos down my bell-bottom jeans" A photograph here would be really good to give an illustration of the style. To show what was typical of the counter culture or hippie influenced style at that time. She mentions lots of shops names and places. Car model, highway and price of gas. From these facts one can assemble a picture of how affluent young people were at that time and how far they were prepared to drive, or hitch hike as her husband did. This is comparable to our lifestyle today and therefore seems familiar and not forty years ago. However it is an important historical record as it illustrates many events surrounding a concert trip at that time. A simple thing like buying earrings has meant something to the person that is why it is remembered. Consider if this was the record of a journey in Britain made by the wife of an occupying Roman in 122, AD. This was the time when Hadrian's Wall was built. Every small detail is important because it gives us information about how daily life was at that time. What Lynne has described is part of the story, part of the record and her description of Neil Young the Mountain man collaborates with Thomas's description: "Tattered jeans, scruffy mocs, faded flannel, hair covering his glorious eyes before the wickedest grins, harmonica, guitar, piano" There are many parallels between Thomas and Lynne's story verifying the actual process of following or getting into Neil Young. Even though Thomas and Lynne's situations are vastly different, they both belong to a big part of the youth culture that was moving in a common direction at that time. The 'mocs', are moccasins and it is probably standard Neil Young checked flannel shirt (faded flannel). The instruments Neil Young was playing were the standard ones at that time as can be seen in a BBC film of his concert in England. Here he is dressed all tatty that makes him seem vulnerable and unable to look after himself. The wickedest of grins is typical Neil and the comments like " Neil Young and the gate-crashes" help him to bond with the audience and give a sense of intimacy.[106] **Mark, wrote April 6th , 2009**: "Neil Young January 14th , 1973, Buffalo NY. I was 16, and my older brother and I caught N in Buffalo on ...... The most memorable song for me was Dance, Dance, Dance, a song I was familiar with from the Collector's Item bootleg. I'm sure some of the appeal was the fact that it's three chord structure made it one that I could play easily on guitar but also the fact that it was an unreleased tune made it special. Curiously enough LA, also a unreleased song from the show, had less impact on me Alabama also stands out from the concert. My brother, as hard core Stone freak, appreciated Borrowed Tune with its line of "I'm singing this borrowed tune/I took from the Rolling Stones". We didn't catch the stolen melody being more captivated by the lyrics, but once Dale Anderson mentioned it in his newspaper review it became obvious. A few other things from the concert come to mind. While waiting for the show to begin a beach ball was being batted around (a common enough occurrence during the time) but it careened towards the stage and fear struck me as it made a path towards one of those beautiful Martin guitars. I envisioned the beach ball knocking over the Martin to an echoing crash, dinging the vintage instrument but blessedly the trajectory wasn't right for such a collision. Somebody in the audience stomped on a drink cup and the ensuing pop explosion through the arena. Concerts in the Auditorium were frequently marred by boneheads setting of firecrackers (smuggled in from nearby Crystal Beach, Canada) and the pop had a similar sound, drawing the ire of much of the audience. This was Neil and there was no place for such stupidity. The way Neil stomped his feet, alternating between left and right to mark time during Harvest. He was sitting down during the acoustic portion of the show and my seats to the right of the stage offered a limited view of him, mostly of the patches on his jeans. During the electric portion of the show my vantage point wasn't much of an issue as Neil moved forward and frequently crossed the stage. The next opportunity I had to see Neil Young in concert was on August 11th 1974, with Crosby, Stills, Nash and Young. This was at an all day, outdoor concert held at the football stadium. Also on the bill were Jesse Collin Young and Santana. David Crosby was just off stage right during the Santana set visibly enjoying the show and Neil's dog, Art was (and his handler) were stage left for the CSNY set. This show had less of a concert feel for me. More of a be there on a summer day, less concentrated attention to the music. Our seats were distant and the sound was thinner than I like (although I'm sure it was plenty load on the field just in front of the stage). As such the music became more of a backing track for the day. I wish I could say I heard stellar versions of "Love Art Blues" or "Don't be Denied" that day but musically the only things I recall with clarity were Stephen Stills' acoustic rip through of "You Can't Catch Me/Word Game" and the trippy "Pushed It Over the End". This however benefited from the vastness of the stadium. From my seat I was subject to the grandest echo chamber in the world. Guitar solos (especially the one just before the bridge) hit me and then bounced back from the end of the stadium adding brittle support to the surrealism of the song's vibe. The wash of sound was an audio tide deepening the "on this lonely shore" section and to the emotional emptiness. The song felt timeless. It is still one of the most transcendent music moments of my life. When the Stills Young band played the Niagara Falls Convention Centre on July 4th, 1976 the atmosphere was started out celebratory. It was the nation's bicentennial and the crowd was primed for flags and fireworks. That was probably the major problem with the show, the aforementioned fashion of tossing firecrackers into the crowd did nothing to unify an already splintered song list. Stephen Stills' Cuban rhythm excursions seemed at odds with Neil Young's hit list. "The Loner" was a standout, maybe because it had both players featured and showed glimmers of the anticipated guitar interplay I hoped to hear. Stills did some Hendrix-like guitar work on the obligatory "Star Spangled Banner" and the band's version of "For What It's Worth" was stellar, partly because of historic value of the song. Stills and Young revamping a Buffalo Springfield song, the importance of the moment was not lost on the crowd. Or at least the part of the crowd there for the music. Both the band and the crowd became irritated by the disruptive element of the crowd (the delicacy of Blackbird was shattered for me by the catcalls) and while it never became outright ugly the general feel of the show ended up being one of "that could have been so much better". Of course given the aborted tour's ending I feel lucky getting to see this band in concert." Mike is someone who really has a tale to tell his grandchildren. He has experienced Neil Young in three seminal events in his career. Namely as a "solo artist," with "Crosby, Stills and Nash" and with the short lived, "Stills, Young Band". He experiences the first Neil Young concert when he was 16, in 1973, and the last event in 1976. This is considered one of the peak periods in Neil Young's career. Marks description brings out the real 'zeitgeist' of the period and as a musician he gives a very clear description of the different music styles: "Cuban rhythm excursions, guitar interplay, Hendrix like guitar work, guitar solos that bounced back from the end of the stadium." Mark was sitting in, "the greatest echo chamber in the world." And observes how Neil was keeping time with his feet, by stomping them alternatively between left and right. Every Neil Young fan can relate to this kind of moment with an example of a song on record they really love or a live concert experience. I have met some Danish Neil Young fans who were not so fluent in English and when I translated the words for them it really enriched their experience. Without a doubt Neil Young has brought a lot of precious moments to a lot of people all over the world during his career. We probably all take a momentary 'freeze frame' at the opening bars of a familiar Neil young song on the radio and 'remember the days' Mike gives a description of a 'Neil Young moment' where he describes his feelings during the song "On this Lonely Shore" as: "One of the most transcendent music moments of my life." He also mentions Martin guitars, note his concern that they do not get damaged, as he plays guitar himself he is aware of their value, (not just in dollars). Musicians have a special relationship to their Martin guitars. Apart from really capturing the' zeitgeist', his description of dates and locations make them easy to document. According to the Sugar Mountain website[107] the first concert was with Stray Gators at Memorial Auditorium, Buffalo, NY.

NEIL YOUNG UND SEINE ANLEIHE AN DIE METAPHORIK DER UREINWOHNER AMERIKAS

Meine Arbeit beschäftigt sich mit der Musikrichtung Country /Rock in den sechziger Jahren, zu welcher Zeit viele Musiker Bühnenkleidung im Stil des Wilden Westens des 19.Jahrhunderts trugen.

Mein Hauptaugenmerk liegt auf Neil Young, seiner Karriere als Künstler und seinem gewaltigen Einfluss auf die Musikgeschichte, sowohl als Solokünstler als auch als Mitglied verschiedener Formationen.

Besonderes Interesse hat sein Gebrauch von indianischer Kleidung und Symbolen und die damit verbundene von ihm gewünschte Botschaft.

Daneben beschäftige ich mich auch mit anderen Künstlern und der Unterhaltungsindustrie im Allgemeinen und deren Verwendung dieser Symbolik. Ich war bestrebt herauszuarbeiten, wie authentisch diese Symbole waren und in wieweit sie ein zutreffendes historisches Zeitbild repräsentierten.

Ich beginne mit einer gesellschaftlichen Beschreibung der fünfziger Jahre und zeige auf, wie die Ureinwohner in z.B. John Fords Western dargestellt wurden. Das Buch "On the Road" und das Werk des Dichters Gary Snyder trugen auch dazu bei, das Interesse an der indianischen Kultur während der sechziger Jahre zu wecken, ebenso wie die Filme "Easy Rider", "Little Big Man" und "Soldier Blue". Letztere ziehen Parallelen zwischen der Ausrottung der Ureinwohner durch US Truppen im 19.Jahrhundert und Geschehnisse während des Vietnam Krieges. Neil Youngs Protestlieder und die Anti Kriegsbewegung sind deshalb auch von Bedeutung in diesem Zusammenhang.

Die Entwicklung des wachsenden Interesses an der indianischen Kultur veranschauliche ich, in dem ich Neil Young, Nachfahren der Ureinwohner und andere Zeitzeugen anführe.

Ich beschreibe, wie es Neil Young gelang, die Weltanschauung der Hippies, die Konterrevolution und die Epoche der Bürgerrechtler durch seine Musik miteinander zu verbinden.

Im Näheren untersucht meine Arbeit die Bedeutung der Bürgerrechtsorganisation der Ureinwohner Amerikas, AIM genannt und deren Einfluss auf die gesellschaftliche Stellung dieser Menschen.

Neil Young hat durch seine Musik, seine Dichtung und sein Interesse an gesellschaftspolitischen Entwicklungen wesentlich zum Zeitgeist der genannten, höchst interessanten Epoche beigetragen.

BIBLIOGRAPHY.

Bloom, A. (2001). Long Time Gone. London: Weidenfeld & Nicolson.

Castro, M. (1983). Interpreting the Indian. Norman: university of Oklahoma.

Cheewa James (1995) Catch the Whisper of the Wind. Health Communications, Florida.

Corral, M. o. (1966). Great Western Indian Fights. Lincoln: university of Nebraska.

Costner, K. (Instructor). (1990). Dances With Wolves [Film].

Cronyn, G. W. (1991). American Indian Poetry. New York: Fawcett.

Cutler, C. L. (2002). Tracks that Speak. Boston: Houghton Mifflin.

Davis, R. (1995). Strong Hearts. Turin: Apeture.

Debo, A. (2003). History of the Indians of the United States. London: Folio.

Downinmg, D. (1994). Neil Young. A Dreamer of Pictures. London: Bloomsbury.

Echard, W. (2005). Poetics of Energy. Indinana: Indiana University.

Elliott, M. A. (2007). Custerology. Chicago: University of Chicago.

Faragher, R. V. (2007). Frontiers , A Short Hisstory of the American West. New York: Yale University.

Fowler, C. &. (2007). Beyond Red Power. US: School for Advanced Research.

Furay, R. (1998). For What it's Worth. London: Rogan House.

Gallop, A. (2001). Buffalo Bill's Wild West. UK: Sutton Pulisher.

Grant, S. (1998). Essential Neil Young. London: Chameleon.

Heatley, M. (1997). Neil Young in his own Words. UK: Page Brothers.

Heatley, M. (1994). Neil Young. His Life and Music. London: Hamlyn.

Historical Research (21. 02 2008).

Inglis, S. (2003). Harvest. New York: Continuum.

Josephy, A. M. (1970). Red Power. US: American Heritage.

Kane, L. (2003). Ticket to Ride. Philadelphia: Running Press.

Korn, J. (1967). The Cowboys. New York: Time Life.

korn, J. (1973). The Indians. New York: Time Life.

Krise, S. A. (08. September 2008). North American Indians in the Great War. American History .

Larimore, A. G. (1997). First Person, First Peoples. Cornell: Cornell.

Liberty, J. S. (1967). Cheyenne Memories. New Haven: Yale University press.

Lincoln, K. (1997). Native American Renaissance. Los Angelse: University of California.

Marwick, A. (1998). The Sixties. Oxford: Oxford.

McDonough, J. (2003). Shakey. London: Vintage.

Miller, D. H. (1992). Custer's Fall. The Native American Side of the Story. New York: Meridian.

Morrison, J. (1987). From Camelot to Kent State. New York: Times.

Neihardt, J. G. (1961). Black Elk Speaks. Lincoln: Univesity of Nebraska.

Nelson, E. H. (2001). Telling Stories. US: Peter Lang.

New York Review of Books . (06. 03 2008).

Parkman, F. (1973). The Oregon Trail. London: Folio.

Petridis, A. (2000). Neil Young . Kill Your Idols. New York: Thunders Mouth Press.

Prats, A. J. (2002). Invisible Indians. Cornell: Cornell University.

Rolling Stone Magazine (1968, 1969, 1970).

Richards, Keith. (2010) Life, New York: Little Brown.

Rogan, J. (1982). Neil young. London: Proteus Books.

Rogan, J. (2001). Zero to Sixty. London: Calidor.

Slotkin, R. (1998). Gunslinger Nation. Oklahoma: Oklahoma University.

Williamson, N. (2002). Neil Young . Journey through the Past. San Francisco: Backbeat Books.

young, N. (1974). Complete Music Vol. 1. Secaucus: Warner Bros.

Young, N. (1975). Complete Music Vol.2. Secaucus: Warner Bros.

Young, S. (2006). Neil and Me. London: McClelland & Stewart.

DVD

BBC Documentry, (2008). Dont be Denied [Film].

BBC Documentry, (2007). Hotel California [Film].

Cash, J. (Instructor). (2000). Johnny Cash, the Man,his world, his music [Film].

Jarmusch, J. (Instructor). (1995). Dead Man [Film].

Jarmusch, J. (Instructor). (1997). Year of the Horse [Film].

Young, N. (Instructor). (2006). CSNY / Deja Vu [Film].

ENDNOTES

[1] The Archives Vol. 1 1963–1972, (box set) Neil Young, released 2009

[2] The Observer 30.05.2010, page 15. Film news on The Death of Hopper

[3] The Word,aug.09,issue 78,p.80

[4] Furay,1997,p.168

[5] Ibid, p. 104

[6] Furay, 1997,p.117

[7] Furay,1997,p.118

[8] www.imdb.com/title/tt0093285/usercomments (Granada TV, 1987, 20 Years ago Today.)

[9] Released in 2009

[10] http://www.itnsource.com/shotlist//ITN/1967/02/08/X08026701/

[11] Bison Park Mecklenburg

[12] Furay, 1997,p.105

[13] Rolling Stone, 1970, April 30,p.40

[14] Furay, 1997,p.105

[15] Uncut, July 2003, cover

[16] Furay, 1997,p.104

[17] Furay, 1997

[18] See Rusties comments

[19] Furay,1997

[20] Released on the Atlantic label in the UK in 1970

[21] John Wesley Harding.

22 http://hyperrust.org/Words/NeilUsesHistory.html

23 www.sacheenlittlefeather.net/

24   Many of these points are made by Kyle Bichan and she is a primary source.

25 http://www.filmsite.org/wild.html

26 http://smartenergygroups.com/samotage/posts/23-Neil-Young-s-LincVolt-an-Electric-1959-Lincoln-Continental

27 Bloom,2001,p.155

28 Furay,1997,p.255

29 Hotel California BBC documentary

30 Slotkin 'Gunslinger Nation'

31 http://en.wikipedia.org/wiki/Hair_(musical)#cite_note-Lortel-5

32 Haun, Harry. "Age of Aquarius", Playbill, April 2009, from Hair at the Al Hirschfeld Theatre, p.7

33 Furay,1997,p.258

34 Keith Richard's 'Life' page 289.

35 Furay, 1997,p 259

36 It's All Right Ma I'm Only Bleeding

37 David Cosby was later forced to leave the band.

38 geocities.com/james_mazzeo/jamesmazzeo.html

39 Spin Magazine, 11, 1995

40 Furay 1997.p.227

41 Furay, 1997,p.230

42 Neil Young Live at the BBC documentary

[43] Furay, 97,p. 227

[44] Rolling Stone,1969,Aug.12,p.12

[45] Rolling Stone,1969 Sept. 20, p.16

[46] Esalen Institute California September 14th 1969 (YouTube).

[47] 1970 Atlantic Records

[48] Released on Vanguard Records 1967

[49] The dog apparently just wandered in as the shot was taken.

[50] Rolling Stone. Dec.27,1969,p.26

[51] Now known as Tom O'Neal

[52] http://www.mountainsonggalleries.com/

[53] http://www.tgoportfolio.com/

[54] April 30, 1970, p.5

[55] Slotkin, 1998,p.520

[56] http://www.tgoportfolio.com/store/index.php?main_page=index&cPath=40

[57] Compiled in 2006

[58] This remark can be heard on the live CSN&Y live album '4 Way Street'.

[59] Harvest Moon, Hank to Hendrix

[60] Marwick,1998,p.59

[61] McDonough, 2003,p374

[62] LP1966, Buffalo Springfield

[63] LP, 1976, Illegal Stills

[64] Don't be Denied, BBC documentary, 2007,

65 The Films of Bud Boetticher, Ride Lonesome 1959. DVD box set, Sony.

66 Sergio Leone 'Spaghetti Westerns'

67 DVD CSN&Y Déjà Vu

68 DVD film Heart of Gold

69 Prats, 2002, p.259

70 DVD Déjà vu 2006

71 Time Life Books, 1995,p.171

72 See, sources , Rusties

73 Marwick. 1997.p. 569

74 Marwick, 1997, p. 216

75Slotkin, 1998, p.579

76 Personal experience (I was at the concert)

77 The Life Magazine (May 15, 1970)

78 Morrison,1987, p. 338

79 Songfacts.com- Ekristheh, Halath, United States

80 Déjà vu DVD

81 Déjà vu DVD

82 Rogan, 2001,p.310.

83 Rogan, 2001,p.312

84 Rogan,2001,p.313

85 Bloom,2001,p.7

86 William Colt MacDonald

[87] Eddie Delang, Larry Markes, Dick Charles

[88] Rogan, 2001,p.498

[89] Rogan, 2001,p.503

[90] Marwick,1998,p 459

[91] Marwick 1998, p.459

[92] Rusties

[93] Furay, 1997, p.211

[94] Furay 1997, p. 133

[95] Furay 1997, p. 158

[96] Furay, 1997, p. 266

[97] Ibib, p.267

[98] TimeLife, 1973,p.24

[99] Furay 1997, p.168

[100] Personal knowledge.

[101] Wikipedia: Chrome Dreams II

[102] KILIradio.org

[103] Rolling Stone Sept.22,2005,p.20

[104] Marwick,1998,p.7

[105] http://en.wikipedia.org/wiki/Topanga,_California

[106] Personal experience

[107] http://www.sugarmtn.org/year.php?year=1973

Stephen M. Catchpole was born within the sound of the Bow Bells.

He grew up in Camberley, Surrey. He went on the road in 1972 and during the next four years travelled extensively in Europe, North Africa and Canada.

He works as a teacher and has two sons. He has an MA in Social Studies from University of North London and a Cand.mag in History from the University of Copenhagen.

www.ingramcontent.com/pod-product-compliance
Lightning Source LLC
Chambersburg PA
CBHW032118280326
41933CB00009B/889